American Values

Other Books of Related Interest:

Opposing Viewpoints Series

Internet Censorship

Multiracial America

War

At Issue Series

Should the Rich Pay Higher Taxes?

Should the US Close Its Borders?

Current Controversies Series

Politics and Religion

Poverty and Homelessness

"Congress shall make
no law . . . abridging
the freedom of speech,
or of the press."

First Amendment to the US Constitution

The basic foundation of our democracy is the First Amendment guarantee of freedom of expression. The Opposing Viewpoints Series is dedicated to the concept of this basic freedom and the idea that it is more important to practice it than to enshrine it.

American Values

David M. Haugen, Susan Musser, and Michael Chaney,
Book Editors

GREENHAVEN PRESS
A part of Gale, Cengage Learning

Farmington Hills, Mich • San Francisco • New York • Waterville, Maine
Meriden, Conn • Mason, Ohio • Chicago

Elizabeth Des Chenes, *Director, Content Strategy*
Douglas Dentino, *Manager, New Product*

For more information, contact:
Greenhaven Press
27500 Drake Rd.
Farmington Hills, MI 48331-3535
Or you can visit our Internet site at gale.cengage.com

Articles in Greenhaven Press anthologies are often edited for length to meet page requirements. In addition, original titles of these works are changed to clearly present the main thesis and to explicitly indicate the author's opinion. Every effort is made to ensure that Greenhaven Press accurately reflects the original intent of the authors. Every effort has been made to trace the owners of copyrighted material.

LIBRARY OF CONGRESS CATALOGING-IN-PUBLICATION DATA

American values / David M. Haugen, Susan Musser, and Michael Chaney, book editors.
      pages cm. -- (Opposing viewpoints)
   Includes bibliographical references and index.
   ISBN 978-0-7377-6945-6 (hardback) — ISBN 978-0-7377-6946-3 (paperback)
   1. Social values—United States. 2. United States—Moral conditions. I. Haugen, David M., 1969– II. Musser, Susan. III. Chaney, Michael, 1949–
HN90.M6A446 2014
306.0973—dc23

2013049845

Printed in the United States of America
1 2 3 4 5 6 7 18 17 16 15 14

Contents

Chapter 3: Should Americans Promote Patriotism?

Chapter 4: Can American Values Bridge Cultural Divides?

Why Consider
Opposing Viewpoints?

> *"The only way in which a human being can make some approach to knowing the whole of a subject is by hearing what can be said about it by persons of every variety of opinion and studying all modes in which it can be looked at by every character of mind. No wise man ever acquired his wisdom in any mode but this."*
>
> *John Stuart Mill*

In our media-intensive culture it is not difficult to find differing opinions. Thousands of newspapers and magazines and dozens of radio and television talk shows resound with differing points of view. The difficulty lies in deciding which opinion to agree with and which "experts" seem the most credible. The more inundated we become with differing opinions and claims, the more essential it is to hone critical reading and thinking skills to evaluate these ideas. Opposing Viewpoints books address this problem directly by presenting stimulating debates that can be used to enhance and teach these skills. The varied opinions contained in each book examine many different aspects of a single issue. While examining these conveniently edited opposing views, readers can develop critical thinking skills such as the ability to compare and contrast authors' credibility, facts, argumentation styles, use of persuasive techniques, and other stylistic tools. In short, the Opposing Viewpoints Series is an ideal way to attain the higher-level thinking and reading skills so essential in a culture of diverse and contradictory opinions.

In addition to providing a tool for critical thinking, Opposing Viewpoints books challenge readers to question their own strongly held opinions and assumptions. Most people form their opinions on the basis of upbringing, peer pressure, and personal, cultural, or professional bias. By reading carefully balanced opposing views, readers must directly confront new ideas as well as the opinions of those with whom they disagree. This is not to argue simplistically that everyone who reads opposing views will—or should—change his or her opinion. Instead, the series enhances readers' understanding of their own views by encouraging confrontation with opposing ideas. Careful examination of others' views can lead to the readers' understanding of the logical inconsistencies in their own opinions, perspective on why they hold an opinion, and the consideration of the possibility that their opinion requires further evaluation.

Evaluating Other Opinions

To ensure that this type of examination occurs, Opposing Viewpoints books present all types of opinions. Prominent spokespeople on different sides of each issue as well as well-known professionals from many disciplines challenge the reader. An additional goal of the series is to provide a forum for other, less known, or even unpopular viewpoints. The opinion of an ordinary person who has had to make the decision to cut off life support from a terminally ill relative, for example, may be just as valuable and provide just as much insight as a medical ethicist's professional opinion. The editors have two additional purposes in including these less known views. One, the editors encourage readers to respect others' opinions—even when not enhanced by professional credibility. It is only by reading or listening to and objectively evaluating others' ideas that one can determine whether they are worthy of consideration. Two, the inclusion of such viewpoints encourages the important critical thinking skill of objectively evaluating an author's credentials and bias. This evaluation will illuminate an author's reasons for taking a particular stance on an issue and will aid in readers' evaluation of the author's ideas.

It is our hope that these books will give readers a deeper understanding of the issues debated and an appreciation of the complexity of even seemingly simple issues when good and honest people disagree. This awareness is particularly important in a democratic society such as ours in which people enter into public debate to determine the common good. Those with whom one disagrees should not be regarded as enemies but rather as people whose views deserve careful examination and may shed light on one's own.

Thomas Jefferson once said that "difference of opinion leads to inquiry, and inquiry to truth." Jefferson, a broadly educated man, argued that "if a nation expects to be ignorant and free . . . it expects what never was and never will be." As individuals and as a nation, it is imperative that we consider the opinions of others and examine them with skill and discernment. The Opposing Viewpoints Series is intended to help readers achieve this goal.

David L. Bender and Bruno Leone,
Founders

Introduction

> "The patriots of 1776 . . . gave to us a re-
> public, a government of, and by, and for
> the people, entrusting each generation to
> keep safe our founding creed. And for
> more than two hundred years, we have."
>
> US President
> Barack Obama,
> second inaugural address,
> January 21, 2013

In his January 21, 2013, second inaugural address, President Barack Obama asserted that the values on which the United States was founded must be preserved and remain the guiding principles by which the nation moves forward. Using the US Constitution as a platform to describe the unique character of the United States, the president argued, "What makes us exceptional—what makes us American—is our allegiance to an idea articulated in a declaration made more than two centuries ago: 'We hold these truths to be self-evident, that all men are created equal; that they are endowed by their Creator with certain unalienable rights; that among these are life, liberty, and the pursuit of happiness.'" Obama claimed that the country cannot embrace the future if it relinquishes its duty to upholding these rights.

According to the president, Americans prove equal to the task of securing these rights because of the strength of the principles embodied within them. "Our celebration of initiative and enterprise, our insistence on hard work and personal responsibility, these are constants in our character," the president remarked. Focusing on the power of collective action over self-interest, Obama depicted a country that strives to ensure that all citizens are treated equally, that all have a place in the nation's economy, and that all share in the prosperity of a society dedicated to expanding privileges and safeguarding rights for every individual. "That is our generation's task," Obama stated, "to make these words, these rights, these values of life and liberty and the pursuit of happiness real for every American."

How to make these rights "real" comprises the main arguments of the president's speech. In Obama's view, the nation must bring to a close its decade of "perpetual war," it must grow its middle class, it must temper its free markets with reasonable regulations, it must protect the misfortunate through collective welfare, it must defend the rights of women and minorities, and it must offer hope to immigrants who—like the foreign masses who helped shape the country—see the United States as a land of opportunity. Calling on Americans to support these ideals, the president concluded, "You and I, as citizens, have the power to set this country's course. You and I, as citizens, have the obligation to shape the debates of our time—not only with the votes we cast, but with the voices we lift in defense of our most ancient values and enduring ideals."

Greg Sargent of the *Washington Post* reported his thoughts on the speech in an article published in the immediate wake of the address. "Obama made the case for still more progress in the arena of civil rights—and for expanded progressive governance to combat inequality and protect our 'citizens' from economic harm—by grounding it directly in the nation's founding values." For Sargent, the conflating of "founding values" with an exhortation to collaborative action allowed the president to lay out "an expansive philosophical blueprint today that liberals now have the opportunity to hold him to." The speech insists that this is how the United States has conducted itself from its inception, and this is how its future course will be determined if it adheres to these ideals.

Of course, not all Americans believe in the agenda President Obama laid out in his speech. Some might agree with the constitutional principles but not the manner in which these principles were connected to specific policy issues. In a quick response to the second inaugural address, Ron Rodash of PJ Media simply stated, "The president took generalities with which we all agree and used them to imply that to carry on in the American tradition, 'progressive' measures favored by his base need to be implemented." What Rodash and some other critics note is that, in speaking of the necessity of rules in a fair market economy and a commitment to Medicare, Medicaid, and Social Security, for example, the president's rhetoric aligned these controversial notions with the values presumably set forth in the early days of the nation's conception. Many conservative commentators argue that these issues are not the legacies of the Founding Fathers but, instead, are opposed to US values of free enterprise and individual liberty. Writing for Breitbart News on the day of the inauguration, Joel B. Pollack maintains that by blaming the rich for social injustices and putting forth an agenda that redistributes the nation's wealth, Obama's speech "was a declaration of political war on individual liberty."

The reactions to the president's second inaugural address demonstrate that Americans' national values are subject to interpretation. Some may attest that the country stands together for "life, liberty, and the pursuit of happiness," but the definitions of these admittedly vague and controversial terms have much to do with the perspective of those who employ them rhetorically and little to do with any connections to agreed-upon absolutes. *Opposing Viewpoints: American Values* affirms that the ideals of the nation are subject to debate—or at least their application to public policy and social mores. In the following chapters: What Values Are Important to the United States?, Are American Values Threatened?, Should Americans Promote Patriotism?, and Can American Values Bridge Cultural Divides?, authors contest some of the key values that pervade national discourse. Some social critics and politicians maintain that the country's values are, as President Obama argues, "constants in our character," while others claim that our national character has always been changing, so these "constants" must always be reappraised as the times demand. Even the president, in his second inaugural address, acknowledged that, in regard to life, liberty, and the pursuit of happiness, the nation remains on "a never-ending journey to bridge the meaning of those words with the realities of our time." This anthology illustrates how this "one nation" continually revisits its founding principles in order to clarify their meaning in the present age.

OPPOSING
VIEWPOINTS®
SERIES

CHAPTER 1

What Values Are Important to the United States?

Chapter Preface

In the 2012 release *The State of Our Unions: Marriage in America*, the Institute for American Values (IAV) and several partner organizations warn that the debate over same-sex marriage, the rise of serial partnerships, and the growing disinterest among young people for permanent unions between man and woman suggests that the value for marriage in the United States is on the decline. "Why should we care?" IAV asks. "Marriage is not merely a private arrangement; it is also a complex social institution. Marriage fosters small cooperative unions—also known as stable families—that enable children to thrive, shore up communities, and help family members to succeed during good times and to weather the bad times." To this organization, marriage is an important social bond that holds together the country's middle class and helps shape the American Dream.

As respect for marriage falls into decline, IAV states, the nation will become a society of winners and losers. Children of educated parents—who are more apt to form and stay in stable marriages, according to the institute—will follow their parents into more successful and financially secure futures, while their less-educated peers will suffer the economic and familial hardships of broken marriages or uncommitted cohabitation that seem to plague this demographic. Middle America, which used to be comprised of married working families, the institute contends, is becoming increasingly defined by undereducated single parents or broken homes. The significance for future generations is captured in the institute's claim that "today's children of Middle America are growing up without stable families to help them weather economic change, deregulation, and globalization."

If economic security is the aim of marriage, however, some critics have taken issue with the notion that the US working poor are failing to live up to that standard. In a June 25, 2013, article for *Forbes*, Trevor Butterworth cites experts who insist government spending on marriage education for the poor has been useless or simply misallocated. Butterworth draws upon a 2012 UCLA study that indicated that the lower income families didn't need such education because "it turned out that the poor not only value marriage just as much as those with more income, they actually have *a better grasp* of the values needed to make a marriage work than wealthier people." According to the research, the poor were focused on acquiring a job, achieving a livable income, and putting money aside in savings because, as lead author and social psychologist Benjamin Karney states, "Being able to make ends meet is important to marriage."

IAV and the UCLA research team place importance on the value of marriage—in this case, the financial stability that grows the nation's middle class and promotes childrearing practices that ensure its continuation. Whether that core value is imperiled remains a point of contention for those who seek to understand the widening of the income gap and the problems facing working class America. In the following chapter, social critics examine values associated with national identity.

| "*Freedom of religion is a cornerstone of the American experiment.*"

Religious Freedom Is Necessary for American Values to Flourish

Jennifer A. Marshall

In the following viewpoint, Jennifer A. Marshall argues that the freedom of religion guaranteed by the First Amendment is still necessary for the United States to function properly and lead the rest of the world by example. Marshall traces the historical roots of the freedom of religion clause to show that the founders believed this freedom would work to limit the government from growing too large. While the founders opposed a federally mandated religion, Marshall contends that individuals like Thomas Jefferson felt that the exercise of both public and private religion would serve to guide the morality of the nation and lead the people to create a successful country. Marshall serves as director of the Richard and Helen DeVos Center for Religion and Civil Society at the Heritage Foundation.

As you read, consider the following questions:

1. According to the viewpoint, what percentage of Americans view religion as at least "somewhat important"?

2. As stated by the author, what did Thomas Jefferson mean when he advocated a "separation of church and state"?

3. What international agreement does the author identify as guaranteeing religious freedom as a fundamental human right worldwide?

Religious liberty and a thriving religious culture are defining attributes of the United States, characterizing the American order as much as its political system and market economy. From the earliest settlements of the 17th century to the great social reform causes led by religious congregations in the late 19th century and again in the 20th century, religion has been a dominant theme of American life.

Today [December 10, 2010], almost 90 percent of Americans say that religion is at least "somewhat important" in their lives. About 60 percent are members of a local religious congregation. Faith-based organizations are extremely active in providing for social needs at home and in sending aid abroad.

Why does religious liberty matter—to America and to the world?

Freedom of Religion Limits Government Power

Freedom of religion is a cornerstone of the American experiment. That is because religious faith is not merely a matter of "toleration" but is understood to be the exercise of "inherent natural rights." As [the first US president] George Washington once observed: "[T]he Government of the United States, which gives to bigotry no sanction, to persecution no assistance, requires only that they who live under its protection should demean themselves as good citizens in giving it on all occasions their effectual support." And "what is here a right towards men, is a duty towards the Creator," James Madison [the fourth US president] wrote in his 1786 *Memorial and Remon-*

strance. "This duty is precedent, both in order of time and in degree of obligation, to the claims of Civil Society."

The model of religious liberty brilliantly designed by Madison and the other American Founders is central to the success of the American experiment. It is essential to America's continued pursuit of the ideals stated in the Declaration of Independence, the ordered liberty embodied in the Constitution, and peace and stability around the world.

The key to America's religious liberty success story is its constitutional order. The Founders argued that virtue derived from religion is indispensable to limited government. The Constitution therefore guaranteed religious free exercise while prohibiting the establishment of a national religion. This Constitutional order produced a constructive relationship between religion and state that balances citizens' dual allegiances to God and earthly authorities without forcing believers to abandon (or moderate) their primary loyalty to God.

This reconciling of civil and religious authorities, and the creation of a Constitutional order that gave freedom to competing religious groups, helped develop a popular spirit of self-government. All the while, religious congregations, family, and other private associations exercise moral authority that is essential to maintaining limited government. The American Founders frequently stated that virtue and religion are essential to maintaining a free society because they preserve "the moral conditions of freedom."

Public Religious Engagement Was Encouraged by the Founders

Today, the religious roots of the American order and the role of religion in its continued success are poorly understood. One source of the confusion is the phrase "separation of church and state," a phrase used by President Thomas Jefferson in a widely misunderstood letter to the Danbury Baptist Association of Connecticut in 1802. Many think this means a

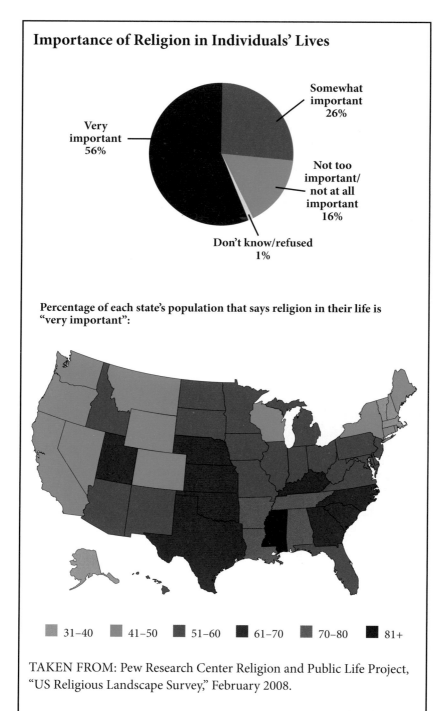

Importance of Religion in Individuals' Lives

Very important 56%

Somewhat important 26%

Not too important/ not at all important 16%

Don't know/refused 1%

Percentage of each state's population that says religion in their life is "very important":

31–40 41–50 51–60 61–70 70–80 81+

TAKEN FROM: Pew Research Center Religion and Public Life Project, "US Religious Landscape Survey," February 2008.

radical separation of religion and politics. Some have gone so far as to suggest that religion should be entirely personal and private, kept out of public life and institutions like public schools.

That is incorrect: Jefferson wanted to protect states' freedom of religion from federal government control and religious groups' freedom to tend to their internal matters of faith and practice without government interference generally. Unfortunately, Jefferson's phrase is probably more widely known than the actual text of the Constitution's First Amendment: "Congress shall make no law respecting an establishment of religion, or prohibiting the free exercise thereof."

The American model of religious liberty takes a strongly positive view of religious practice, both private and public. While it does not mean that anything and everything done in the name of religious liberty is not subject to the rule of law, it does mean that the law ought to make as much room as possible for the practice of religious faith. Far from privatizing religion, it assumes that religious believers and institutions will take active roles in society, including engaging in politics and policy-making and helping form the public's moral consensus. In fact, the American Founders considered religious engagement in shaping the public morality essential to ordered liberty and the success of their experiment in self-government.

Religious Freedom Breeds Good Governments

Defying predictions that political and social progress would eventually marginalize religion, religious belief and practice remain widespread and vibrant around the world.

"The very things that were supposed to destroy religion—democracy and markets, technology and reason—are combining to make it stronger," write the authors [John Micklethwait and Adrian Wooldridge] of a book [*God Is Back: How the Glo-*

bal Revival of Faith Is Changing the World] about religion's persistence in culture and politics around the world.

In this era—as in all prior human history—God has occupied the thoughts of man. Conscience, the mystery of existence, and the prospect of death challenge every human being to grapple with questions of transcendence and divine reality.

Religious freedom recognizes the right of all people to pursue these transcendent ends. This right is granted not by government but by the Creator. By respecting it, a government acknowledges that such ultimate issues are outside its jurisdiction, and that conscience is answerable to a higher authority than the law of the land. Individuals and institutions should be free to believe and to act in response to divine reality.

Because religious liberty is the bedrock for all human freedom, it provides a sturdy foundation for limited government. Liberty of conscience demands, and ultimately justifies, limited government.

Conversely, limited government requires individual responsibility. Freedom engages the moral responsibility of each and every person. In a free society, religion is an ally of good government as it forms the moral character of individuals and communities.

Religious freedom is a fundamental human right that ought to be enjoyed by the people of all nations. This principle has been recognized in the 1948 Universal Declaration of Human Rights and subsequent international agreements. Despite widespread recognition, many people are unable to exercise this basic liberty.

Even with religion's global prevalence, religious freedom is far from universally respected. About a third of the world's nations restrict religion to a high or very high degree, according to the Pew Forum on Religion & Public Life. Seventy percent of the world's population lives in these countries.

In some cases, totalitarian governments have oppressed religious individuals and groups generally. In others, statist regimes built on an established religion have persecuted religious minorities.

Countries designated by the U.S. State Department as "countries of particular concern" because they restrict religious freedom (such as North Korea, Iran, and Burma) suffer in other ways as well. They also tend to have the least economic liberty—and some of the worst economic outcomes.

On the other hand, governments that respect religious liberty tend to respect other freedoms as well. Religious freedom is strongly related to political liberty, economic freedom, and prosperity. As one researcher of international religious liberty [Brian Grim] notes, "[W]herever religious freedom is high, there tends to be fewer incidents of armed conflict, better health outcomes, higher levels of earned income, and better educational opportunities for women."

The 1998 International Religious Freedom Act made religious liberty an official part of U.S. foreign policy. The United States committed to promote freedom of religion as "a fundamental human right and as a source of stability for all countries" and to "identify and denounce regimes" that engage in persecution on the basis of religion.

American Religious Freedom Is a Model for the World

Condemning and curtailing religious persecution is a critical goal, but religious freedom includes much more. Our vision of religious liberty must be robust.

Attempts to relegate religion to private life or to prevent religious institutions from conducting their business according to their beliefs threaten this fundamental freedom. Religious individuals and institutions should be free to exercise their religious belief within their private spheres as well as to engage publicly on the basis of religion. Believers should be free to persuade others to embrace their beliefs. Individuals should be able to leave or change their religion without fear of reprisal, and all should have the right to protection under the rule of law regardless of belief.

The most secure and consistent protection for religious liberty needs to be rooted in constitutional government. U.S. public diplomacy can support the development of such robust religious freedom by telling America's success story.

That requires that U.S. policymakers understand and be able to articulate the role of religion in the American constitutional order. In the 21st-century war of ideas, U.S. public diplomacy must rely on the bedrock of American founding principles in the fight against potent ideologies that present strong, coherent, and deeply misguided explanations of the nature and purpose of human existence. Evaluating religious dynamics around the world should become a regular function of analysis, and articulating the role of religion in the U.S. should be a consistent feature of communications strategy.

Religion and traditional morality continue to play a significant role in American public life. Most Americans continue to attach great significance to religious faith and practice, marriage, family, and raising children in a morally rich and supportive environment—values shared in many highly religious societies around the world.

Religious freedom is the birthright of all people, but too few governments around the world acknowledge it and far too many people have never enjoyed it.

One of the gifts of providence to the United States is a Constitution that has successfully safeguarded this fundamental right. It is a gift Americans should cherish and a model for all throughout the world.

> *"Open secularity is increasingly seen— especially among young people—as a way of making a personal statement in a contentious culture."*

Why Secularism Is Good for the US

David Niose

In the following viewpoint, David Niose explains that secularism in the United States is increasing, especially among young people. He attributes this to the fact that the secularist movement in the United States has evolved into a response to the pervasiveness of religion in public life. He argues that atheists have been traditionally overlooked in the United States but believes that things are changing and notes that atheist groups on college campuses are growing in number. He sees the modern secularist movement as a way for young people to take a stand against the fundamentalist element in politics. Niose is a writer and president of the American Humanist Association.

As you read, consider the following questions:

1. According to the Gallup poll cited by the author, what percentage of Americans under thirty would accept an atheist political candidate?

2. Why, in Niose's opinion, did groups like the American Civil Liberties Union, which oppose the religious Right, appoint religious leaders in the past?

3. To what does the author attribute the rise of the modern secularist movement?

Secular Americans are on the rise, and all Americans—religious and nonreligious—should take note. The secular community, fueled by increasing numbers of Americans who are stepping away from religion and aided by online tools that weren't available to prior generations, has quickly become a social and political movement, as open secularity is increasingly seen—especially among young people—as a way of making a personal statement in a contentious culture.

According to a recent Gallup report, for the first time ever a majority of Americans—54 percent—would now vote for a qualified atheist for president. Nobody is predicting that the country will soon be electing a chief executive who refrains from saying "God bless America," but the unmistakable trend is in the direction of tolerance, and even admiration, of personal secularity. In fact, the same survey shows that acceptability of an atheist candidate rises to 70 percent among Americans under 30.

This helps explain the booming growth of the Secular Student Alliance (SSA), the national umbrella organization for college atheists, which has expanded from just a few dozen campus affiliates in 2007 to over 350 today. The SSA is now moving into high schools, where secular student groups will surely do much to normalize atheists in grassroots America.

Unlike previous generations, young people today are more likely to consider religious skepticism an important part of their personal identity, viewing open secularity as a way of expressly rejecting the agenda of the Christian right. There may be many ways of telling the world that you are appalled by right-wing attacks on birth control, environmental regulation, and education, but few do it more efficiently than the simple statement, "I'm an atheist."

As such, the booming secular movement can best be understood as a response to the pervasive influence of religious conservatism in American public life. Indeed, although secular activists like to describe their movement in terms of what it stands for—reason, critical thinking, science and ethics—it can also be seen as a new strategy for fighting back against politicized religion.

Opponents of the fundamentalist agenda have had few successes since Jerry Falwell's newly formed Moral Majority helped elect Ronald Reagan in 1980, so surely a new opposition strategy was needed. Because of the Christian right's success—and its opponents' failure—religiosity is more widespread in politics and government than ever, as candidates for high office frequently deny evolution, discuss their faith in detail, hold prayer rallies, and even claim that church-state separation is a myth. Most of this would have been unthinkable a generation ago.

To understand why old strategies of opposing the religious right failed, we need only compare them to those of today's secular movement. In a speech discussing the rise of politically active religious conservatism in 1983, Senator Edward Kennedy was quick to discuss his own religion. "I am an American and a Catholic," he said. "I love my country and treasure my faith." This mantra—that the religious right has no monopoly on religion, and that liberals can be religious too—was a constant theme emphasized by politicians fighting against the Moral Majority and its successors.

Major advocacy groups opposing the religious right in the 1980s and 1990s were also quick to emphasize religious connections. Television producer Norman Lear formed People for the American Way in 1981 as a direct response to politically engaged religious fundamentalists. The ACLU and Americans

A Secular State Is Less Judgmental than a Secular Individual

A secular individual lives in *"le siècle"* (this world), in time and history, and does not believe in the "eternal." He thinks religion is an illusion, and might even consider that it is a *dangerous* illusion, so that the world would be better off without religious people, priests, etc. Provided he does not prevent other people from thinking and acting differently, he has the right to think that religion is, as the young [German philosopher and economist Karl] Marx said, "the opium of the people." On the other hand, the State is secular if it does not refer its acts to a super-human entity. It does not affirm that the latter exists or does not exist, and has nothing to say about its meaning, form, sacred texts, etc. That State remains in the secular realm but respects all creeds provided they can be accorded with the basic tenets of liberal democracy.

Guy Haarscher, "Religious Revival and Pseudo-Secularism,"
Cardozo Law Review, *vol. 30, no. 6, June 2009.*

United for Separation of Church and State were also in the early forefront in combating Falwell and the Christian right. These groups appointed religious leaders as board members and officers, enabling them to credibly insist that the religious right had no monopoly on religion.

All of these opponents fought valiantly against the fundamentalist agenda, but their approach was missing one critical element. That is, with all of the major opposition to the religious right stressing its own religiosity, religion was of course being given undue exaltation. This meant that America's secular demographic—a sizable and valuable population—was being completely marginalized.

With the benefit of hindsight, we can now see that this played directly into the hand of the Christian right. If the assumption in politics was that religion must be elevated in importance, religious conservatives were guaranteed stature in almost any policy debate, just as nonbelievers were sure to be ignored.

While there is of course nothing wrong with occasional reminders that liberals can be religious, the troubling success of the religious right has caused many to rethink the strategy of overlooking the secular demographic. Indeed, many who seek rational public policy now see their own personal secularity as a quality to be emphasized, not downplayed.

This explains the rapid growth of the modern secular movement, and its potential for success in fighting back against the religious right. The contemporary secular movement is a new form of social-political activism that challenges politically engaged fundamentalists from an entirely new direction. Rather than rushing to show that they can be religious too, today's secular activists assert that they aren't impressed by claims of religiosity. They are good Americans, and they are demanding that public policy be discussed on a level that is rational.

Secular Americans will also point out that there is no justification for prejudice against nonbelievers. Numerous studies show that social ills—violent crime, teen pregnancy and many others—correlate more strongly to religious populations than to secular. This holds true within the United States (comparing religious regions to more secular) and internationally (comparing relatively religious America to more secular societies).

Nonbelievers, of course, have always been part of the American landscape, but only recently have they begun to realize that open identification is a way of making a statement, of standing up against the fundamentalist element in politics. As they become more visible, their hope is that reason will return to the public arena.

| "*Capitalism also creates more wealth for those on the lowest rung of the income ladder than any other system.*"

Capitalism Promotes Freedom

Robert Ringer

In the following viewpoint, Robert Ringer asserts that Americans have been taking freedom, and the capitalist economy that accompanies it, for granted. He worries that the United States could be at a tipping point where socialism, and then communism, could take hold, due to the fact that people have become accustomed to government handouts. The one factor that has prevented this conversion so far, in Ringer's opinion, is the drive to maintain the capitalist system, but as this drive subdues coinciding with the increased reliance on government assistance, the country risks losing its freedom. The author holds firm in his belief that capitalism is the only system that can counter this fall, create prosperity for all people, and decrease reliance on the government, making it a system he believes all Americans should fight to maintain. Ringer is a New York Times *best-selling author and host of the Liberty Education Interview Series.*

As you read, consider the following questions:

1. According to the author, who were Karl Marx and Friedrich Engels, and what did they say about socialism?

2. In considering socialism, what does the Ringer say people do not take into account?

3. How, in the author's opinion, has the United States been able to avoid a violent revolution like the ones Marx and Engels referred to?

Americans are easy prey when it comes to political distraction debates. The [National Labor Relations Board] NLRB's outrageous attempt to block Boeing from opening a new plant in South Carolina is a distraction. Proposed card-check legislation is a distraction. Our obsessive meddling in Middle Eastern countries is a distraction.

All these are important issues, but they are merely subcategories of the foundational issue that Americans should be focused on: loss of freedom. In a truly free society, none of these issues would even arise, because they are outside the scope of human freedom.

Unfortunately, instead of freedom, we are being cleverly engineered into social-justice automatons by left-wing zealots who run Atlas Shrug-like bureaucracies [like those written about by author Ayn Rand in her novel *Atlas Shrugged*] such as the Environmental Protection Agency, the National Labor Relations Board, and the Department of Education, to name but a few of our worst enemies from within.

The antithesis of freedom is communism. [German philosopher and economist] Karl Marx and his lackey benefactor, [German social scientist] Friedrich Engels, firmly believed that violent revolution was the only way to bring about pure communism, and that such a revolution was possible only where capitalism existed. Capitalism, they insisted, was a necessary ingredient for creating a wide financial disparity between workers and the privileged class.

I'm still baffled as to why Marx and Engels would want to increase the income disparity between the classes, only to rectify the disparity through violent revolution. Sounds like an-

© Nik Scott / CartoonStock.com

gry, left-wing mischievousness to me. Perhaps it was based on their knowledge of the utter failure of the French Revolution, which had led only to mob violence, unthinkable human carnage, and, ultimately, a Napoleonic dictatorship.

But the fact is that there has never been a communist revolutionary threat in capitalistic societies such as Japan, Taiwan, or (pre-China) Hong Kong. The most notable communist revolutions have occurred in Russia, China, Vietnam, and Cuba, none of which could have been considered capitalist countries at the time. Thus, Marx and Engels would have considered the United States to be a perfect crucible for testing their convoluted class-warfare theories.

Socialism Is the First Step Toward Communism

Of course, only naïve dreamers believe in the communist fairy tale that under communism, the state will eventually "wither away" because there will be so much of everything for everybody that government will no longer be necessary. But I do believe that Marx and Engels were on to something with their belief that socialism would precede communism. In fact, they referred to socialism as a "transitional stage of society" between capitalism and communism.

Nevertheless, here in the U.S. we have long suffered from the delusion that "European-style socialism" is a nice, peaceful, cradle-to-grave compromise between capitalism and communism. Elitists on both the right and the left have come to believe that European society is static, and that so long as European countries keep their redistribution-of-wealth policies finely tuned, capitalists will go right on producing enough to support the parasitic masses.

What they have not taken into account, however, is a crucial factor known as *human nature*. Homo sapiens—particularly its progressive subspecies—is, by nature, an avaricious creature. Worse, the more goods and services he acquires without work, the more avaricious he becomes. In fact, the human appetite for wealth without work is insatiable.

The result is that when producers can no longer create enough wealth to appease the voracious appetites of the masses, those on the receiving end become increasingly upset. Which is why the riots we've witnessed in Greece, Spain, Portugal, and Italy are not mysterious events. On the contrary, they were predictable decades ago.

If a man has spent his whole life believing it is his right to retire at age fifty-eight, and someone else's obligation to support him in his retirement in the lifestyle to which he has become accustomed, he is incapable of comprehending that he must work until—Gasp!—age sixty.

It was just as predictable that rioting would come to the United States. Madison, Indianapolis, Columbus, and other state capitals [where labor unions protested in 2011] are but a mild preview of what the U.S. can expect once the invisible depression becomes visible even to those who are still in a Keynesian coma.

The United States Is Ripe for a Communist

With the coming debt-ceiling increase, no cutbacks in store for Social Security or Medicare, and a majority of politicians unwilling to make serious spending cuts in other unconstitutional, redistribution-of-wealth programs, my view of what's on the near horizon is pretty clear. I see the (admitted) unemployment rate at 25 percent or more, housing prices collapsing at least another 50 percent, the DJIA [Dow Jones Industrial Average of stock prices] free-falling several thousand points in a single day, and inflation rising to 30 percent, 40 percent, or perhaps even higher.

All of which would set the stage for the cherished uprising that Marx and Engels so passionately longed for—and that [US president] Barack Obama and his Marxist pals believe they are near to achieving. The reason the United States has been able to avoid violent revolution until now is because even through the eras of the most left-leaning presidents and Congresses of the past hundred years, there was always enough pushback to keep capitalism alive. But that pushback has been rapidly declining, and is now coming from only 50 percent or less of the population.

There's an irony in the fact that Marx and Engels believed capitalism was necessary in order to create more wealth disparity. The irony I'm referring to is that capitalism also creates more wealth for those on the lowest rung of the income ladder than any other system, so income and wealth disparities, while interesting phenomena for academic eggheads to ponder, are irrelevant. The only thing that's relevant is how well off each individual is in absolute terms—*not* in comparison to others.

The bottom line is that without capitalism, there is no such thing as prosperity for the masses. Capitalism is freedom in its purest form. Thus, without freedom, capitalism, by definition, cannot exist, because it is nothing more than a subcategory of freedom—the freedom to trade one's goods and services with others without interference from government.

If you agree with most of what I've said in this [viewpoint], you should make it a point to vote only for those office seekers whom you are convinced truly understand that the main threat we face is our loss of freedom. My pessimistic vision of the future would change substantially if pro-freedom types were able to win the presidency and overwhelming majorities in both houses of Congress in 2012. The optimistic side of me hopes it will happen, but my realistic side keeps reminding me that history has not been kind to those who put their trust in politicians.

> *"Communism and Nazism controlled
> people with fear. We control people
> with economic bondage."*

Capitalism Promotes Enslavement

Robert J. Dewar

In the following viewpoint, Robert J. Dewar recounts his experiences working in corporate America as the basis for his argument that capitalism has failed to create the innovation and improvements it promises and instead works only as a system of control and enslavement. Dewar uses two examples, one from Procter and Gamble and one from Ford Motor Company, to show that capitalism only allows those who do what they are told and follow company policy to get ahead. Additionally, Dewar insists that this system creates "prisoners" out of employees and encourages poor workmanship. These experiences lead the author to conclude that capitalism, just like communism and Nazism, is just a method used by those in power to control everyone else. Dewar worked corporate jobs with various companies, but was so appalled by his experience with Ford Motors that he wrote the book A Savage Factory *to expose what he believed to be the company's poor management and lack of compassion.*

As you read, consider the following questions:

1. What did the author learn he had to do to succeed in his job at Procter and Gamble?

2. What did the author find happened when he worked for Ford Motors and "tried to find men not working"?

3. How is capitalism similar to and different from communism and Nazism, according to Dewar?

Years ago, when I was growing up, one of my best friend's father told me there is not a nickel's difference between any of the "isms." All of them find a way to control the working people to keep them working to support a handful of filthy rich white guys at the top of the pyramid. It took most of my life to realize that he was right.

Oh, yes. I was raised on "god bless America because we are free." I was ready to go marching off to protect us from the hordes of 'godless communists' who would spread the red tide over all the world, stealing away our precious freedom. I was taught that if you work hard and a get a good education it will be rewarded, and you, too, can take your place beside the handful of filthy rich white guys at the top. I guess I was 30 or so before I began to question the accuracy of these suppositions.

To Succeed in Corporate America You Must Fit In

My first job after earning an MBA, where I learned that to get rich you have to use "OPM" (other people's money), and you have to learn to manipulate people, was at Procter and Gamble [P&G]. The seed of doubt was planted in graduate school. They did not teach the value of hard work, honesty, and being debt free. They taught that if you want to be one of the filthy rich white guys it was stupid to work hard. What you had to do was finesse your way into power structures, borrow up to your eyeballs so you could rub elbows with the elite, and, while you were glad handing them at a cocktail party, learn to stab them in the back and take what they have. But this seemed more like how the Nazis or Communists operated. Weren't we superior to them because we achieved freedom by working hard and following the golden rule?

At P&G I saw capitalism in action. But it was not like the system that I learned about growing up. I quickly learned that hard work had nothing to do with moving up the ladder, nor did ability or education. It was all about fitting in, and nothing else. To succeed you had to become a good Proctoid, also known in the hallowed halls of P&G as the "Corporate Master Race." If you became a good Proctoid you did not have to work hard, or be very smart, or accomplish much. All you had to do was fit in, not rock the boat, learn when and how to speak, and live, act, and dress like a good Proctoid. If things did not make sense to you, but were entrenched in the corporate culture, it was neither smart nor safe to point these things out.

I went back to my reading. Wasn't being a good Proctoid a whole lot like being a good Communist or a good Nazi? Didn't both of these isms condition people to fit in and not ask questions or challenge the prevailing culture? Didn't they have penalties for asking the wrong questions or stepping out of line? I did not want to be a good Nazi, a good communist, or a good Proctoid, so I quit and went to Ford Motor Company. At Ford I found honesty and openness the very first day on the job.

Capitalism Has Not Led to Innovation

My boss had a sit down with me and explained that the UAW [United Automobile, Aerospace and Agricultural Implement Workers of America Union] was a pack of lazy, lying thieves who cheated Ford out of an honest day's work on every shift. My job would be to catch them, write them up, and fire them.

Inequality in the US Economy Can Be Overcome

The U.S. economy, as presently constituted, produces tremendous inequality, insecurity, and overwork. Nor is there reason to think that growing from a $14 trillion to, say, a $20 or $25 trillion economy will change these destructive trends.

It doesn't have to be this way. There is no inherent reason why we could not cease to regard more income as a good in itself, but instead alter our political economy so that it provides what Americans really need and want: greater employment security, stronger protection against the pitfalls of poverty, and more free time. We could choose to have the public guarantee employment opportunities for every willing worker, to put a floor on income, to decommodify health care and education, to reduce the gross inequalities of income and status which themselves help fuel consumerism, and to take future productivity growth in the form of more time, not more stuff.

Thad Williamson,
Dollar and Sense, *May/June 2008.*

My job was to be a super prick, and then the UAW would fear me, and that would intimidate them into doing the jobs they were paid to do. I had learned at P&G not to ask the wrong questions, so I went out on the manufacturing floor to be the super prick that Ford was paying me a king's ransom to do.

What I learned was that the more I tried to find men not working, the more they did not work. It seemed to me that if we wanted them to work we had to treat them like human beings and not prisoners of war. I discussed this with my boss and he accused me of "collaborating" with the work force. Ford wanted an "us versus them" mentality in the auto plants, which made no sense to me.

Another thing that did not make sense was the quality of the cars we were building. It was terrible. We received the largest recall in automotive history for transmissions that had killed over 200 people. I understood why the quality was bad. It was bad because the work force "got back" at Ford for being treated like jail inmates. But mostly it was bad because Ford wanted it to be bad so people would get sick of paying for repairs and would buy a new car. This did not seem like the capitalism that I had learned about.

The capitalism I had learned about would result in constant innovations and quality improvements because corporations would compete against each other and the ones who made the best quality would win. Was I the only one who picked up this concept in school? Why are products getting worse instead of better? Do you remember the appliances and vehicles and clothing from 50 years ago? All of it was better than what can be purchased today. A Hoover sweeper from 1920 is far superior from a Hoover sweeper from 2009. Has capitalism failed?

Capitalism Controls People Like Communism and Nazism

The communists conditioned people from birth to be good communists. Hitler conditioned Germans to be good Nazis from a very young age. We condition people from birth to be good consumers. We teach them, subconsciously, that what they have defines how important they are. So they spend their lives working to buy things they don't need that constantly break down so they will be "normal" to their peers and feel good about themselves. Communism and Nazism controlled people with fear. We control people with economic bondage. In all three systems the handful of filthy rich white guys at the top keep their positions through mass thought control. All that differs is the control techniques that they use. My friend's father was right. There is not a nickel's difference between any of the isms.

> *"If democracy is 'a folk's participation in its own destiny,' we can conclude that America, without a folk, has no destiny."*

Democracy Is Not Possible in the United States

Jared Taylor

In the following viewpoint, Jared Taylor outlines the multitude of ways in which democracy is flawed, from its failure to truly implement a representative government, to its reliance on money for power, to its risk of creating tyranny. He makes the case that each situation can be observed in the US system. Ultimately, he states, the US democracy will fail because its citizens have no real connection with their citizenship or their country, making them unable to create meaningful bonds with each other that would lead to good governance. Taylor is editor of American Renaissance, *an online magazine that examines how race impacts individuals and society.*

As you read, consider the following questions:

1. When and where was the earliest parliament in the West established, according to Taylor?

2. As stated by the author, what is the result of winners in modern politics beating their opponents by narrow margins?

3. What is the main difference between modern democracy and ancient Greek democracy, according to the author's reading of Alain de Benoist?

There may be no better place or time to meditate on the defects of democracy than the United States in 2013. What an absurd figure we cut in the world, as we try to impose on Afghans and Iraqis a form of government utterly alien to them, while our own rulers lurch from crisis to failure back to crisis.

Alain de Benoist, one of the sharpest thinkers of the French Right, wrote *The Problem of Democracy* in 1985, but its insights are as fresh as ever. . . .

The Term Democracy Is Misunderstood

Mr. de Benoist has written as powerful a critique of democracy as one is likely to find—so powerful that it is almost a surprise to find that he concludes with a prescription for how democracy could be made to work. Needless to say, both his critique and his prescription, though rivetingly relevant to the United States, are unknown in this country.

Mr. de Benoist begins by pointing out that "democracy" is so mystical a term that virtually every government on earth claims to be "democratic." The communist countries of East Europe were "democratic republics," and African dictators claim to be democrats.

Westerners generally think democracy—loosely defined as free participation by the people in public life—is unquestionably the best form of government. Mr. de Benoist argues that no form of government is best for all countries at all times. Democracy, moreover, is European and heavily influenced by the Enlightenment and Christianity (an organization of celibate priests could not have hereditary offices, so voting was essential to church government). The leftist idea that the whole world should embrace democracy is pitiably ethnocentric.

Nor, as is commonly argued, is Western democracy a recently evolved and therefore particularly advanced form of government. The oldest parliament in the West, the Icelandic Althing, was established in [AD] 930, and there were clearly democratic tendencies in the ancient Italian republics, the Hanseatic municipalities, and the charters of the Swiss cantons.

Nor is it accurate to find stark differences between democracy and despotism. Unlike the Orientals, Indo-Europeans have seen very little despotism. In [Homer's epic poem] the *Iliad*, in ancient Rome [753 BC to AD 1453], in Vedic India [a time when the earliest scriptures of Hinduism were written beginning sometime between 1700 and 1100 BC and ending between 500 and 150 BC], and among the Hittites [people living in Anatolia during the eighteenth century], there were popular assemblies that decided civil and military matters. In the West, kings were elected, and monarchy did not become generally hereditary until the 12th century. Even then, kings shared power with elected parliaments. In the West, virtually every system has therefore been a mix of collective and solitary rule. Some would even call the Athenian system not so much a democracy as an extended form of aristocracy.

Democracy Is a Dictatorship of Mediocrity

Mr. de Benoist notes that it has long been common to scoff at the idea of letting ordinary people have a role in government. As [French critic and historian] Hyppolyte Taine (1828–1893) wrote, "Ten million ignorant men cannot constitute a wise one." Ernest Renan [a French philosopher and writer] (1823–1892) wrote that elections mean a "destiny committed to the caprice of an average of opinion inferior to the grasp of the most mediocre sovereign called to the throne by the hazards of heredity." [French author] René Guenon believed that "the opinion of the majority cannot be anything but an expression of incompetence."

The best known American exponent of this view was [journalist and culture critic] H.L. Mencken, who wrote, "If it were actually possible to give every citizen an equal voice in the management of the world ... the democratic ideal would reduce itself to an absurdity in six months. There would be an end to all progress."

Many people therefore call democracy a dictatorship of mediocrity. Since politicians must appeal to the masses, elections throw up third-rate men. And because politicians must be reelected they never think in the long term and can never take necessary but unpopular steps.

In a democracy, the majority is supposed to rule, but Mr. de Benoist notes that this is an expression of numbers, not wisdom. "Quality cannot stem from quantity," he writes. "The idea that authority, a quality, may stem from numbers, a quantity, is rather disturbing."

A majority vote is supposed to reflect the sovereign will of the people, but Mr. de Benoist is skeptical of a sovereign will that expresses itself as half the votes cast, plus one. Moreover, majorities are constantly shifting; does that mean the will of the people is constantly shifting? If so, are the people competent to rule? Nor does majority rule take intensity of feeling into account; the vote of a coin-flipper counts the same as that of a passionate partisan.

A different approach is to claim that the majority view is the absolute and permanent will of the people—so long as it is one's own view. On this theory, anyone who expresses a contrary view can be exterminated. This was [Russian Communist leader Vladimir] Lenin's and [French revolutionary Maximilien de] Robespierre's version of democracy.

In these less philosophical times, a majority vote is seen as just a tool, a transient statistic that permits government to operate, rather than a significant expression of the people's will. Modern democracies accept the idea of permanent pluralism and the proliferation of parties. But this concedes that there is no real voice of the people; only clashing factions, none of which seeks the national good.

When there are many parties there is never a majority—only shifting, unstable coalitions—which means impotence and irresponsibility. Whether there are many parties or few, parties become ends in themselves. Their survival, along with their hangers-on, becomes more important than whatever ideas they once represented.

No matter what is claimed in democracy's name, it is actually a system of rule by minorities, since only elected officials actually rule. Moreover, they routinely break their election promises and are always free to flout the wishes of their constituents. Mr. de Benoist writes that when a voter hands over his decision-making power to a representative, "he is making use of his liberty only to renounce it." This legitimizes the power of politicians over a passive population.

Even [Genevan philosopher] Jean-Jacques Rousseau scoffed that "the English people thinks it is free; it is greatly mistaken, it is free only during the election of members of Parliament; as soon as they are elected, it is enslaved, it is nothing."

Money Rules Politics

At the same time, money rules politics. A poor man can hardly become a candidate, much less win an election. And because having power is the best way to raise money, the political class perpetuates itself. Moreover, Mr. de Benoist notes that "the tyranny of money clearly goes hand-in-hand with corruption and financial scandals." Money proves the bankruptcy of the process itself: Most of it is spent on television advertising, which is the most insulting form of political discourse.

That voters can be swayed by television advertising only shows how powerful the media are. As Mr. de Benoist notes,

"Popular will is thus being increasingly fabricated by using methods to condition public opinion."

This makes fools of the sovereign people:

> The fact that elections may be free is meaningless if opinion-forming is not. . . . Only a small number of people hold opinions that may be regarded as genuine convictions. The vast majority of people have no real opinions, but only impressions . . . for they are shaped by events, propaganda, and various forms of conditioning.

The candidates themselves are caught in the same snare. Modern political platforms are often based on surveys, which give everyone the same result. Therefore, writes Mr. de Benoist, "Out of demagogy and a concern to please, candidates all end up saying much the same things to everyone."

And what they say is mundane rubbish: "In a society pervaded by the ideal of egalitarianism, the very notions of grandeur and collective destiny raise suspicion." American politics, in particular, is all talk of money, spending, and budgets. It is the language of bookkeeping, not of destiny, greatness, or overcoming.

A Lack of Real Choice Creates Apathy

In modern politics it is common to win by narrow margins. This means no party or politician has a real mandate, and so cannot implement a program. It means politicians always try to win over their opponents' supporters, which again leads to numbingly uniform policies.

This means that "voters are free to opt among different parties because they are prevented from opting among different ideas—for these 'different' parties are increasingly *reasoning* all in the same way."

As a consequence, "Western man has never been more rightfully indifferent towards the 'liberties' he enjoys—although his illusion of having these liberties shackles his will to rebel."

Although voters may be unable to articulate their frustration, sham choices are one of the great sources of today's voter apathy. It is only natural that voter participation declines, and even important offices are won with pitifully small percentages of eligible voters. And who benefits from voter apathy? A self-perpetuating political class that is increasingly protected from discerning and motivated voters.

Voters therefore almost never vote "for," but "against." In a democracy, people are supposed to choose candidates who embody their will and desires. Instead, they vote against candidates who most clearly flout those desires.

As Mr. de Benoist explains:

> Democracy has changed. It was initially intended to serve as a means for the people to participate in public life by appointing representatives. It has instead become a means for these representatives to acquire popular legitimacy for the power which they alone hold. The people are not governing through representatives; they are electing representatives who govern by themselves.

Mr. de Benoist writes that far from being exercises in sovereign power, "elections are a ceremony for bestowing legitimacy: the people crown a candidate or consecrate a president without having much choice in the matter."

Democracy Can Lead to Tyranny

How do defenders of democracy answer their critics? Mainly by arguing that despite its defects, democracy is a government of limited powers and can never subject the people to tyranny. This is false. Any system of government can lead to tyranny. We already live under a "soft" despotism that would be the envy of Louis XIV or Ivan the Terrible. No king could make his subjects account for every penny of income and then dictate exactly what percentage to hand over in taxes. No "absolute" monarch ever told his subjects where they could have a

Democracy Is Pessimistic About All People

The common belief that democracy springs from an eternal optimism about human nature—"trust the people"—needs therefore to be stood on its head. Democracy alone acts on a bleak view of human nature by spreading power as widely and thinly as possible in order to prevent large-scale misuse of it and by having competing forms of selfishness neutralize each other. Hence, there is in America the rivalry horizontally among the executive, legislative, and judicial branches of the federal government and vertically among federal, state, and local entities.

With its distrust of all people, then, democracy represents the application of the idea of original sin to politics. The paradox is that democracy, which is in many ways a secular form of government, turns out to be the only system to implement this central Christian doctrine, while the elitist forms of governance during the Christian Middle Ages did not. Those theocentric societies, by implicitly placing faith in Emperor and Pope, in King and Ayatollah, in unelected aristocrats and clergy, were ultimately optimistic about *some* people, while democracy is actually pessimistic about *all* people.

Manfred Weidhorn, Midwest Quarterly, *Spring 2013.*

smoke, or tell him how long his employees were to work. Our government even claims the right to kill American citizens overseas without a trial; it need only call them "enemy combatants."

As Mr. de Benoist observes, "it is not the idea of 'absolute power' which democracy rejects, but rather the idea that such power may be the privilege of a single person."

Nor is democracy clearly superior to what Westerners dismiss as "dictatorship." Would Singapore be a better, happier place with Western-style elections and political squabbling? Would China? Is Algeria, which has been ruled since independence by a single party, more poorly governed than India? Was Spain under [Francisco] Franco any worse than the current wreck?

Westerners claim that even if Singapore or China have dramatically improved living standards, their systems are inferior because the people do not have free speech. Mr. de Benoist lays bare this hypocrisy. Many European countries ban speech that might "stir up racial hatred," and others even forbid dissident commentary on certain historical events.

Mr. de Benoist notes that if "stirring up hatred" were grounds for muzzling citizens, Communists and socialists should be the first targets, since their vocation is stirring up class hatred. He argues that any brisk attack on a political opponent could "stir up hatred," and that a consistent application of "hate speech" laws would outlaw all political speech. The West makes a fetish of certain subjects and treats them just as hysterically as "dictators" treat criticism of the regime—and for the same reasons.

Mr. de Benoist notes that Germany even bans specific political movements, of both the Right and Left:

> [This requires] believing that the ruling system is so excellent that once it has been established, we have the right to proscribe all possibilities of choosing a different one. All radical dissent—which is to say, all genuine dissent—is thus banned. But can we still call this a democracy?

Democracy Fails Without Citizens

After this blistering critique, what is left of democracy for Mr. de Benoist to support? To answer that question he takes us back to ancient Greece. He notes that in Athens, each citizen had an equal voice in the *ekklesia* or assembly, but emphasizes that "the crucial notion here is not equality but citizenship." Slaves had no voice, not because they were slaves but because they were not citizens, and almost without exception, the only way to become a citizen was to be born of an Athenian mother and father.

As Aristotle pointed out, Athens came first and citizens were born into it. Mr. de Benoist notes that "this view stands in contrast to the concept of modern liberalism, which assumes that the individual precedes society and that man, *qua* individual, is *at once* something more than just a citizen."

Thus, the main difference between ancient Greek democracy and our own is not what are always told: that theirs was direct democracy whereas ours takes place through elected representatives. Instead, we have completely different conceptions of society:

> Ancient democracy defined citizenship by one's origin, and gave citizens the opportunity to participate in the life of the city. Modern democracy organizes atomized individuals into citizens, primarily viewing them through the lens of abstract egalitarianism. . . . The meaning of the words "city," "people," "nation" and "liberty" radically changes from one model to another.

Mr. de Benoist continues:

> The effective functioning of Greek democracy, as well as of [ancient] Icelandic democracy, was first and foremost the result of cultural cohesion and a clear sense of belonging. The closer the members of a community are to one another, the more likely they are to have common sentiments, identical values, and the same way of viewing the world and social ties, and the easier it is for them to make collective decisions concerning the common good without the need for any form of mediation. Modern societies . . . have ceased to be places of collectively lived meaning.

Mr. de Benoist writes that modern democracy that ignores the crucial element of peoplehood is an American invention.

It is no accident that it sprung up among people who do not even have a word that is the equivalent of *Volk* in German or *popolo* in Italian. It is democracy without *demos*.

Mr. de Benoist dislikes the all-men-are-created-equal phrase of the Declaration but, if anything, dislikes even more the idea that men are endowed by their Creator with unalienable rights. The rights that matter in a democracy, he writes, do not come from God but from citizenship and common heritage. The American conception is doomed from the start because "where there is no folk but only a collection of individual social atoms, there can be no democracy."

Democracy Should Give People the Chance to Be Equal

He quotes [French philosopher] Raymond Polin (1910–2001) on the only proper basis of government:

> The source of its legitimacy lies with the body of principles on which the deep-seated consensus of the nation is based. . . . Resting on a given conception of man, of society and politics, this deep-seated consensus carries an obligation to build the future history of the nation according to the inspiration of its spirit.

Mr. de Benoist believes that a healthy democracy transcends rivalries:

> In this context, one should not underestimate the importance of the genuine phenomenon of national and folk consciousness, by means of which the collective representations of a desirable socio-political order are linked to a shared vision, comprised of a feeling of belonging that presents each person with imperatives transcending particular rivalries and tensions.

Under these circumstances democracy provides the fairest way to ensure that elites are genuinely worthy. And democracy does not try to make people equal; only to give them an equal chance to be unequal.

In such a democracy citizens would take an active part in public life, and with modern technology their democracy could be almost as direct as Athenian democracy. People would be active in local affairs and vote in frequent plebiscites and referenda. As Mr. de Benoist writes, "The people should be given the chance to decide wherever it can; and wherever it cannot, it should be given the chance to lend or deny its consent."

The actual mechanisms of democracy—which readily degenerate into the spectacles of vulgarity by which America elects its President—are much less important than citizen participation. Mr. de Benoist believes that a genuinely constituted people could embody [German cultural historian] Moeller van den Bruck's (1876–1925) definition of democracy: "a folk's participation in its own destiny."

The United States Is Missing the Ingredients for Democracy

For American readers, *The Problem of Democracy* throws a harsh light not only on our political system but on even the theoretical possibility of reform. Every one of Mr. de Benoist's criticisms of democracy applies to the United States—and every one of his conditions for its success is missing.

Americans—fatally infatuated with their illusions—are the very people who should read this book but are the very people who will not. If democracy is "a folk's participation in its own destiny," we can conclude that America, without a folk, has no destiny.

Periodical and Internet Sources Bibliography

The following articles have been selected to supplement the diverse views presented in this chapter.

Jonathan Aitken	"Godless Capitalism," *American Spectator*, November 2008.
Austin Dacey and Colin Koproske	"Against Religious Freedom," *Dissent*, Summer 2011.
Kyle Duncan	"How Fares Religious Freedom?" *First Things: A Monthly Journal of Religion and Public Life*, October 2013.
Peter D. Fromm, Douglas A. Pryer, and Kevin R. Cutright	"War Is a Moral Force," *JFQ: Joint Forces Quarterly*, First Quarter 2012.
Nancy Gibbs	"Real Patriots Don't Spend," *Time*, October 13, 2008.
Gary Gutting	"What Work Is Really For," *New York Times*, September 9, 2012.
Yuval Levin	"Beyond the Welfare State," *National Affairs*, Spring 2011.
Barry W. Lynn	"Religious Freedom," *Human Rights*, January 2013.
Barack Obama	"Changing Hearts and Minds," *Time*, August 18, 2008.
Jamie Raskin	"One Nation Under the Constitution: Reason, Politics, and Morality in the New Century," *Humanist*, November/December 2008.

OPPOSING
VIEWPOINTS®
SERIES

CHAPTER 2

Are American Values Threatened?

Chapter Preface

Between May 25 and June 6, 2012, *The Atlantic* and the Aspen Institute surveyed more than two thousand US citizens about the state of American values. In a June 27, 2012, article for *The Atlantic*, pollster Mark Penn concluded from the results, "America's values are in upheaval, triggered by the advance of technology, prolonged pessimism, and a loss of confidence in major social, political, economic, and religious institutions." Seventy percent of those surveyed agreed that values have been getting worse over the past decade, and 63 percent maintained that the nation overall was headed in the wrong direction. Forty-six percent gloomily predicted that values in the United States would continue to decline over the next ten years.

The survey indicated many contributing factors to the weakening of US moral strength. While more than 60 percent of the respondents claimed Americans' support for freedom of speech and religion is stronger than other countries around the globe, a large section of those polled took issue with the state of religion in the United States and the security of the nation's democratic and economic foundations. Only 44 percent thought the US government was a factor in US superiority, and only 40 percent cited the nation's Christian heritage as a comparative strength. Two-thirds of Americans polled voiced the opinion that the economy was on the wrong track, and only 17 percent agreed with the statement that Wall Street executives share the values of the country at large. Beyond these aspects of the perceived decline, Penn notes that those surveyed "point to political corruption, increased materialism, declining family values, and a celebrity-obsessed culture as the culprits."

According to Penn, the survey results were not entirely pessimistic. Besides reaffirming a belief in constitutional values, Americans showed greater tolerance for new ideas and people of different cultures. Penn believes this is a reflection of American youth growing up in a society that has publically deplored prejudices. In addition this younger demographic has weathered economic disaster and witnessed its elders flailing in attempts to promote free enterprise as a cure for the disparities between rich and poor. In Penn's words, "Young people are diverging from their fathers and grandfathers with new attitudes that revolve less around competition and more around equality." Whether this will remain a trend in the future, Penn is unsure. He claims the values of youth might change with age, implying that the present social and economic conditions might be a temporary influence or might signal a lasting change in the nation's direction.

In the following chapter, several authors examine whether specific traditional values in the United States are under threat from fluctuations in the country's social and economic structure. For some, change equals needed progress, while others believe such conceptions of progress veer too much from US moral centeredness. Penn insists, "America's values make sense for a socially maturing country," but not everyone acknowledges that these growing pains are an indication of maturity. As the viewpoints in this chapter attest, American exceptionalism can be defined by its conservative adherence to foundational principles or by its tolerance of and adaptation to changing moral climates.

| *"Somewhere we've shifted from honoring success to envying it."*

Big Government Undermines Freedom and Prosperity

Steven Greenhut

In the following viewpoint, Steven Greenhut argues that the United States has gone from a place that respected and admired capitalism to a country where many people hold a negative view of capitalism because of the increase in the size of government. He contends that some individuals in the media and government attempt to portray the free market as a necessary evil and the government as the savior. Greenhut counters these views and explains that capitalists in the United States fund ideas, charities, and even the government that disparages them. He cautions, however, that as state governments grow larger and demand an increasing portion of income from the wealthy, they risk driving their benefactors to other states. Greenhut is the California columnist for the San Diego Union-Tribune.

As you read, consider the following questions:

1. According to the author, what are some of the investments made by capitalists that show that they are not "mainly greedy people"?

2. What are the problems Steven Greenhut sees with the government and its programs?

3. If taxes are raised too high on people, what does the author suggest they will do?

After hearing the criticism directed toward golfer Phil Mickelson for his modest comments about California's highest-in-the-nation tax rates causing him to consider relocating, I was left wondering what country we live in. Did you ever have one of those moments?

"If you add up all the federal and you look at the disability and the unemployment and the Social Security and the state, my tax rate is 62, 63 percent," Mickelson said. "So I've got to make some decisions on what I'm going to do." He pointed to "drastic changes" that are driving his decision—an obvious reference to the income-tax hikes California voters placed on millionaires like him. Media and public critics were aghast and mocked this poor rich guy for his complaints.

The spectacle of Mickelson apologizing on Sunday [January 20, 2013], then doing so a second time later in the week, was the worst part of this spectacle. "I think that it was insensitive to talk about it publicly to those people who are not able to find a job, that are struggling paycheck to paycheck," Mickelson said. To the AP reporter, Mickelson wasn't sufficiently apologetic: "He didn't apologize for what he said, only that he said it."

Mickelson is just trying to get his mind back in golf, so I don't begrudge him for using the lingo that our society requires from the chastened. It's now "insensitive" for a wealthy person to complain about a confiscatory tax rate as long as there are other, less fortunate people out there somewhere. That's not a healthy attitude in a free and prosperous society.

Opinions of Capitalists Have Changed over the Years

"A generation ago, the vitriol his comments triggered would have been surprising, and somewhat isolated," CalWatchdog's Chris Reed argued. "Griping about taxes used to be something of an American tradition. No more." This attitude, he notes, now comes from the highest level of government.

Consider the president's [Barack Obama] second inaugural address, which was a celebration of the wonders of government. The Democrats who run our state view private business as something ranging from a blight to a necessary evil that can be endlessly tapped to fund every new program they envision.

If you think the "blight" comment is an exaggeration, consider this: Recently, the California Air Resources Board [CARB] sent out a press release celebrating a $300,000 fine it imposed on a business. The quotation from CARB's chief enforcement officer included this warning: "All business owners should pay attention to this case." That's like something uttered by a villain in an Ayn Rand [Russian-American author and founder of objectivism] novel.

I've always sensed a deep understanding that transcends left and right in America—you can make it big and enjoy the fruits of your labor. During the early days of the labor movement, the hard leftists never made much headway because of that deep-seated idea that, no matter how humble one's beginnings, an American can make it big someday.

Something has changed, even as our society has become wealthier. Sure businesses have to comply with regulations and millionaires need to pay taxes, but somewhere we've shifted from honoring success to envying it, from viewing government as a limited tool to achieve a few necessary things (infrastructure, enforcing the rule of law) to seeing it as the be-all and end-all of our society.

Big Government Breeds Crony Capitalism

Crony capitalism is a by-product of big government because the more government is involved in an economy, the more the profitability of business depends on government policy. Even entrepreneurs who prefer to avoid cronyism are pushed into it because they must become politically active to maintain their profitability. When the government looms large in economic affairs, firms and other organized economic groups push for government policies that will help them and try to prevent the harm that is caused by government policies that work against them. If one's competitors are engaging in cronyism, trying to remain free of cronyism means that those competitors will gain government-bestowed advantages. A well-established academic literature stands behind these conclusions. Crony capitalism is a by-product of big government, so the maintenance of small government is the most effective means of controlling it. More government control of the economy is not the remedy for crony capitalism, but rather its cause.

Randall G. Holcombe,
Independent Review, *Spring 2013.*

Capitalists Keep the United States Running

Why is it assumed by these moralistic Affluence Police that the rich are mainly greedy people who spend their money on luxury goods? Charities and non-profits are funded by wealthy people. Real capitalists invest millions of dollars into ideas and often create good jobs in the process. I have no idea what Mickelson does with his money, but it isn't any of my business. Given California governmental attitudes, one can't blame him for looking elsewhere.

For instance, during a recent Capitol press conference, the *Orange County Register*'s Sacramento reporter asked Gov. Jerry Brown about the spending increases in his supposedly austere budget. Brown joked about there being no hope for Orange County readers, according to a *Register* editorial. Then he mocked "this doctrine that government is the problem," which he said is promoted by the "*Orange County Register* or whoever all these people are."

At the Capitol, the free market is viewed as an arcane joke. Yet I look at everything government does—at all those programs and bureaucracies and entitlements that Brown and Obama prefer. I see enormous debt, corruption, abuses of power, union-enrichment schemes, shoddy services, terrible attitudes, and an endless sea of scandal and greed. Just read the newspapers.

But the scorn should be expected. The state uses a static model for calculating revenues. It assumes that if you raise taxes by, say, 20 percent that the state will get 20 percent more money. In the real world, people move to lower-tax places or work less or hide more of their income, and the government gets 20 percent of a smaller pie.

If wealthy people keep leaving, then the state will have to pare back its budget. Perhaps the backlash against Mickelson is a sign of desperation by those who understand there might be limits to how many golden eggs the geese keep laying.

| *"The choice is between unregulated greed, which leaves none of us free, and responsible, effective leadership that protects our freedom."*

Big Government Protects Freedom and Prosperity

Drew Westen

In the following viewpoint, Drew Westen argues that it is the government's duty to protect American citizens' rights, including freedom, the free market, education, and health care, among others. In order for the government to protect these rights, Westen contends that President Barack Obama must present a coherent narrative about the benefits of a large, progressive government. The biggest challenge to achieving this national understanding, according to the author, is the existing narrative that offers only two choices: the free market and capitalism versus tyrannical government and socialism. Westen believes that only by overcoming this dichotomy and convincing the American people of the positive role of big government will the country be able to achieve the highest level of governance and success. Westen is a psychology professor at Emory University in Atlanta and founder of the strategic messaging consulting firm Westen Strategies.

As you read, consider the following questions:

1. What does Westen identify as the biggest difference between progressives and conservatives?

2. According to the author, what is the alternative to "government for the sake of big business"?

3. What are some of the best roles of government listed by Westen?

In his September [2009] speech on healthcare to a joint session of Congress, [US president] Barack Obama invoked the spirit of [former Massachusetts senator] Ted Kennedy to make some modest steps toward almost, sorta, kinda saying that maybe we ought to rethink the role of government.

Unfortunately, since taking office Obama has largely reinforced the conservative "brand" made so popular by Ronald Reagan. In explicitly discussing the role of government in a recent Meet the Press appearance, Obama offered a juxtaposition that would have made Reagan proud: "How do we balance freedom with our need to look after one another?"

In fact, perhaps the biggest difference between progressives and conservatives is that one believes that government inherently infringes on freedom and the other believes that government creates the conditions for it.

If there was a silver lining to the state of the union Obama inherited from his predecessor, it was that George [W.] Bush and the Republicans had so thoroughly discredited the ideology of unregulated greed and hands-off government in matters of financial security that at no time since 1933 was the public more ready for a new narrative about what government should and shouldn't do.

Americans were so frightened and angry about what was happening to their 401(k)s [retirement plans], their housing values (if they still had a home), their health insurance (if they still had or could afford it), their inability to know which of their kids' Chinese toys was filled with lead and the fine

Bigger Government Is Not More Corrupt Government

Despite the—at least—theoretical appeal and coherence of the argument holding that big government should be expected to be bad government, reality seems to tell a very different story. That is, if we take a deeper look into the empirics of the real world, the relationship between government size and corruption seems to run in quite the opposite direction than the one predicted by neo-classical economic theory. Thus, the comparatively least corrupt countries—to a significant extent situated in the northern parts of Europe—have generally much larger governments than the most corrupt ones (generally situated in the developing world, and particularly in sub-Saharan Africa). In fact, the ten least corrupt countries in the world according to Transparency International's ranking (i.e., Finland, Denmark, New Zealand, Iceland, Singapore, Sweden, Canada, Luxembourg, Netherlands, and the United Kingdom) on average collect 23.64 percent of their GDP [gross domestic product] in taxes, while the ten most corrupt countries for which there is data available collect only 14.5 of their GDP in taxes [according to the World Bank].

Anna Persson and Bo Rothstein, Annual Meeting of the
American Political Science Association, September 1–4, 2011.

print in their credit card bills that they were ready for a progressive alternative to the mantra "Government is the problem, not the solution."

The President Needs to Offer a Progressive Narrative for the Country

There is probably still time to begin offering that narrative. But the president needs to recognise that the pragmatic problem-solving that Americans so desperately want from their government presupposes a coherent narrative about the role of government. And he needs to recognise that the direction that problem-solving takes us (e.g., either toward health-care reform that cuts into the profits of pharmaceutical and insurance companies and offers some variant of Medicare as at least one choice to people under 65, or toward reform that taxes and ultimately eliminates the better plans offered to working Americans by their employers) depends on which narrative you offer.

It isn't hard to construct one (FDR [President Franklin Delano Roosevelt, who served from 1933 to 1945] wrote a pretty good rough draft [the New Deal policy established many government security net programs such as Social Security]), but the president needs to tell it—and tell it over and over, until it can compete with the well-branded conservative narrative. A progressive narrative that could move the political centre the way Roosevelt did isn't that difficult to tell: we've been told for years that we face a choice between the free market (capitalism) and tyrannical government (socialism) when that's not our choice at all. The choice is between unregulated greed, which leaves none of us free, and responsible, effective leadership that protects our freedom.

We just saw what happens when we embrace the ideology of unregulated greed—the idea that if we just trust our financial futures to big businesses pursuing their interests, we'll all end up better off. If you want to lose your financial security, your job, your house and your healthcare, it's a great ideology. We just relearned the lesson of our grandparents, who lived through a time when Republicans preached the same philosophy in the run-up to the Great Depression.

The Country Needs Government for the Average Person

The alternative to government for the sake of big business isn't government for the sake of big government. It's government for the average person, who actually creates prosperity by working for a living. No one doubts that we need government to protect our national security. But what we just learned so painfully is that we also need government to protect our financial security—just the way we need government to protect the quality of our air, our drinking water and our bridges and levees. And it's no different for energy, education or healthcare.

Sometimes the best role of government is to partner with business (e.g., to invest in wind and solar energy, so we're not at the mercy of governments that are hostile to us). Sometimes it's to regulate it (e.g., to prevent Wall Street sharks from using our money to speculate away our security—and then expecting us to bail them out and pay them bonuses for their bad judgment). Sometimes it's to compete with big business to make sure the "free market" is really free and competitive and that it extends opportunity and prosperity to all (e.g., in higher education, where our public universities are not only some of the best in the nation but the most affordable, and in healthcare, where the best way to keep insurance companies honest is to make them compete with a plan or two that they don't get to control). Sometimes it's all of the above, and sometimes it's none of the above.

There isn't a piece of progressive legislation the president can pass without making unnecessary concessions to a weak but determined opposition, and without creating tensions within his own party and unnecessarily losing seats in 2010—unless he enunciates an alternative vision of government. Our founders believed we could govern ourselves effectively, and that doing so was the precondition of freedom. Let's prove them right.

| *"There are essential insights that we lose track of when we let 'socialism' be turned into a slur."*

Socialism Coincides with American Values

Jedediah Purdy

In the following viewpoint, Jedediah Purdy argues that the much criticized theory of socialism has multiple, beneficial ideas to contribute to the current discussion on US political and economic challenges, but these ideas are often ignored due to negative misconceptions about the theory. Purdy points out that socialism's take on inequality, economic power, and market characteristics could offer a significant counterbalance to the current policies pervading US politics. More significantly, he maintains that these ideas are not incompatible with American ideals, as critics of the theory would contend. Purdy is a professor at the Duke University School of Law and the author of A Tolerable Anarchy: Rebels, Reactionaries, and the Making of American Freedom.

As you read, consider the following questions:

1. What two big ideas does the author believe are overlooked when socialism is "turned into a slur"?

2. Why is unequal power "bad for democracy," according to the author?

3. What policies does the author state have been implemented due to leaders' judgment that freedom must be protected with democratic control of the economy?

Is socialism's value as a meaningless scare-word played out yet? If so, maybe we can give it a second chance as a real idea. By treating the word as an all-purpose insult, we've lost touch with essential strands of American political thinking.

These ideas were vital to [Presidents] Abraham Lincoln, Woodrow Wilson, and Theodore and Franklin Roosevelt, among others, and were friends, not enemies, to democracy and personal liberty. They aren't usually called "socialism"—Americans have never been big on -isms, left or right—but they add up to an eclipsed tradition that would do the old word proud. Today they might help us make sense of the discontent that has turned Occupy Wall Street [a movement that has organized protests worldwide against social and economic inequality and corruption in business and government] into a national phenomenon—and maybe even do something about it.

Demonizing Socialism Discounts Its Insights

I'm an odd person to make this argument, which I hope is a good thing. I've written books and articles about the good that private property does, and some of my favorite thinkers are Adam Smith (the patron saint of capitalism), Edmund Burke (a touchstone conservative), and Henry David Thoreau (a conscientious would-be anarchist). Temperamentally I'm conservative, and I pretty much agree with Justice Robert Jackson that "the philosophy of the law and the culture of the democratic order come close to being the soul of the American people," and that this is a good thing. But I think there are essential insights that we lose track of when we let "socialism" be turned into a slur.

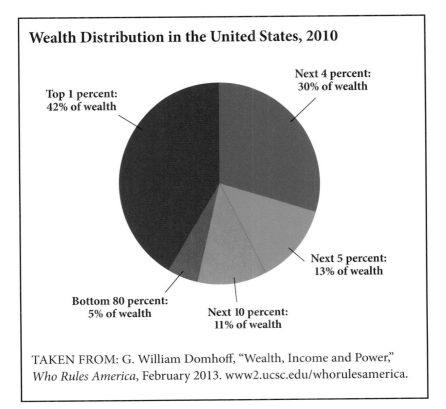

Wealth Distribution in the United States, 2010

Top 1 percent:
42% of wealth

Next 4 percent:
30% of wealth

Next 5 percent:
13% of wealth

Next 10 percent:
11% of wealth

Bottom 80 percent:
5% of wealth

TAKEN FROM: G. William Domhoff, "Wealth, Income and Power," *Who Rules America*, February 2013. www2.ucsc.edu/whorulesamerica.

One big idea is that, in a good country, people should have good work. In the nineteenth century, there was nothing odd or left-wing about this thought. Abraham Lincoln insisted in 1858 that American democracy included a vision of economic citizenship: no one should do degrading work, everyone should have the chance to use both his hands and his mind (otherwise, Lincoln asked, why were we created with both?), and any American who wanted it should be able to earn economic independence. Franklin Roosevelt sounded the same theme in 1932, calling for an "economic bill of rights" that would include the power "to make a comfortable living" for anyone willing to work. [President] Lyndon Johnson's vision of a Great Society, "where the meaning of our lives matches the marvelous products of our labor" was in Lincoln's spirit: the economy should serve the human needs for dignity, personal growth, and connection with other people. Degrading work can undermine all three as surely as no work at all.

Another big idea is that inequality matters. Vast social distance between the wealthy and ordinary people, let alone the poor, undermines the belief that we're all in this together. It's also bad to depend too abjectly on employers or patrons, because dependence undermines self-respect. Franklin Roosevelt made a dramatic gesture in this direction in 1942 when he called for a maximum income of $25,000, but the idea that no one should have to bow and scrape is as old as democracy itself. That's why Aristotle suggested that no citizen should be more than five times richer than another. For more recent evidence that equality and respect touch real human interests, consider public-health research showing that low-rung members of hierarchical organizations get sicker and die sooner than their superiors, regardless of other causes.

Markets Can Threaten Democracy and Personal Freedom

Sometimes markets are the problem and democratic government has to be the solution. During the Depression, no one had to remind Franklin Roosevelt that trusting markets to correct themselves is like assuming that hurricanes don't hit population centers—true in many cases, but a terrible idea in general. Today's lost generations of young graduates and laid-off older workers know economic crises can ruin lives. But after decades of complacent deregulation, in which both parties assumed that sophisticated markets didn't malfunction, we've lost the habit of seeing markets as dangerous. Compare Woodrow Wilson's warning that "there can be no equality of opportunity" unless citizens were "shielded . . . from the great industrial and social processes" that tossed about their lives like so much flotsam.

Even when they work, markets can be enemies to democracy and personal freedom. This is easy to overlook these days. Markets, personal liberty, and democracy together replaced authoritarian socialism in Eastern Europe and elsewhere. It seems natural to see them as permanent allies. But markets, left to their own devices, produce enormous concentrations of wealth. And wealth is power.

Unequal economic power is bad for democracy. Economic power feeds back into the political system, undermining the democratic premise that everyone's vote and voice count the same and tying government to the interests of the wealthy. This abuse of economic power was Theodore Roosevelt's target when he denounced "malefactors of great wealth," and why Louis Brandeis, the great Supreme Court justice, declared that a country could have democracy or great concentrations of wealth, but not both.

Economic inequality also means that personal freedom loses some of its value. More people, regardless of talent and effort, will end up with narrow economic options, all of them bad. Even if they are lightly taxed and regulated, they will be less free, in fact, to do good work and develop their gifts. For this reason, Franklin Roosevelt called concentrated economic power "the despot of the twentieth century." The libertarian economic Friedrich Hayek memorably warned that socialism was a "road to serfdom." Some of the greatest American leaders worried that corporations and the rich could produce serfs of their own. A "more permanently safe order of things," FDR continued, would not hamper individualism, but protect it.

Considering Socialist Ideas Will Strengthen the US Government

Leaders in this tradition judged that some democratic control of the economy is essential to protect freedom, equality, and basic human interests. This has meant aggressive antitrust law to reduce concentrated economic power, strict limits on the role of money in politics, support for unions as an equalizing force in the workplace, safety nets to ensure the independence of even the unlucky or untalented, universally accessible education to make equality of opportunity real, and, yes, redistribution of wealth to level out economic power and keep the society from the fraying of deep inequality.

Many liberals would sign onto a clutch of these policies, but the difference is one of tone: for the Roosevelts and others, these measures were not deviations from the vaunted market, each one requiring elaborate justification and awkward apology. They were essential parts of the social compact. They were designed to achieve real opportunity, meaningful equality, a strong measure of security, and good work for every citizen willing to do her part. They were, in other words, aspects of a political vision that the mainstream of both parties today would denounce, or run from, as "socialism."

Notice that there's nothing here about nationalizing the means of production, the dictatorship of the proletariat, or anything else you may recall from a first-year political philosophy class. The policies associated with these ideas are familiar twentieth-century ones. What's most important now is not any program, but the insights about equality, freedom, work, and power. These ideas are why so much of the twentieth-century program exists in the first place—either because political leaders accepted them, or because leaders were pushed from the left by strong unions and third parties.

You don't have to call yourself a socialist to accept that the country would be better off if we took these ideas seriously. It's always clarifying to have to answer inconvenient challenges. Liberals do better when they defend their work against conservative skeptics, conservatives when they have to argue with optimistic reformers. Similarly, liberals who care about equality, conservatives who care about community, and libertarians who care about personal freedom can also benefit from wrestling with socialist challenges from the American tradition. Everyone cares about these values: socialists have things to say about what they mean and how we can achieve them.

Many American Ideas Are Also Socialist Ideas

It's common to suppose that history has proved socialism can't work because people are selfish and governments abuse power. That is too simple. The twentieth century showed that government without democracy turns tyrannical and centralized economies run off the rails into disastrous inefficiency. These lessons are essential. They don't forbid democratic commitment to American values of equality and good work.

History is full of cause for pessimism, but it is also a pageant of possibility and surprise. From the rise of democracy to the abolition of slavery to the women's movement and gay rights, individual imagination and collective action have created new worlds. These changes have always defied sober and intelligent pessimists, who warned they would be catastrophic. We live in a world that was supposed to be impossible. The cost of success is that now it seems commonsensical.

Since our common sense is built out of the utopian dreams of the past, why not ask whether there is still work to do on Abraham Lincoln's terse definition of democracy: no slaves and no masters? Or on Franklin Roosevelt's call for a strong government that promoted individualism? Or Lyndon Johnson's hope for an America where "the city of man serves not only the needs of the body and demands of commerce but the desire for beauty and the hunger for community"? The idea that markets guarantee freedom, efficiency, and fairness is looking pretty utopian itself right now: these other social visions amount to a dose of reality.

Maybe we Americans will never call ourselves socialists, any more than these presidents did, and that's fine. But, whatever name we give it, we are doing our history a disservice by exiling this tradition just when its concern with inequality, economic power, and the worst tendencies of markets are most relevant. We should revive these very American ideas.

They can help us to articulate our discontent and ask more of our leaders, our economy, and ourselves.

"Unfortunately, over the years it became increasingly evident that welfare did much to discourage marriage and work, and destroy family and community."

America on Welfare

Doug Bandow

In the viewpoint that follows, Doug Bandow makes the case that welfare is bad for America. Bandow says that by increasing welfare programs, America is creating dependent citizens who will think of benefts as rights. The increase in citizens on welfare is starting to cost America not only in the pocketbook, but in its values. Welfare, Bandow claims, is bad for taxpayers and bad for the poor, so reform is desperately needed. Doug Bandow is a fellow at the Cato Institute. A former special assistant to President Ronald Reagan, he is the author and editor of several books, including The Politics of Plunder: Misgovernment in Washington.

As you read, consider the following questions:

1. In this viewpoint, Bandow says the governemnt spends how much a year on antipoverty programs?

2. As stated by the author, how much has federal welfare spending increased since President Obama took office?

3. According to Bandow, what is TANF and how did it impact the welfare system?

Living the good life on welfare. Even the Europeans recognize that they pay a high price for creating an increasingly dependent society.

Denmark has been transfixed by the revelation of a 36-year-old single mother who collects more in benefits than many Danes earn at work, and has done so for two decades. Worried Karen Haekkerup, Minister of Social Affairs and Integration, people "think of these benefits as their rights. The rights have just expanded and expanded."

But it's really not that much different in the U.S., the nominal home of the free. Nearly two decades ago welfare reform briefly captured political attention and won bipartisan support. The effort was a great success. But most welfare programs remained untouched and the gains have been steadily eroded.

Today nearly 48 million people, almost one out of every six Americans, receive Food Stamps. Outlays on this program alone have quadrupled in just a decade. Indeed, the government actively promotes the program, encouraging people to sign up. Other welfare programs also are growing in reach and cost. The Congressional Budget Office recently pointed to "increases in the number of people participating in those programs and increases in spending per participant." The U.S. isn't that far behind Europe.

Indeed, America, like Europe, has a veritable welfare industry. A forthcoming report from the Carleson Center for Public Policy, named after Reagan administration welfare chief Robert Carleson, charges that "The federal government has spawned a vast array of redundant, overlapping and poorly targeted assistance programs." Authors Susan Carleson and

John Mashburn count 157 means-tested programs intended to alleviate poverty. There were more than two score housing programs, more than a score of nutrition programs, almost as many employment/training and health programs, and lesser numbers of cash assistance, community development, and disability programs. More expansive definitions count even more programs—185 total, according to Peter Ferrara.

No surprise, the welfare industry is expensive. Social Security is the single most costly program, but more goes collectively to welfare. Today government at all levels spends around $1 trillion a year on means tested anti-poverty programs. And that amount is just going up and up.

Total federal and state welfare spending rose from $431 billion in 2000 to $927 billion in 2011. Both parties are responsible, but President Obama bears particular responsibility. Last year, explained my Cato Institute colleague Michael Tanner: "Welfare spending increased significantly under President George W. Bush and has exploded under President Barack Obama. In fact, since President Obama took office, federal welfare spending has increased by 41 percent, more than $193 billion per year."

And this is just the start. From 2009 to 2018, figured Heritage Foundation scholars Robert Rector, Katherine Bradley, and Rachel Sheffield, at current rates the federal government will spend $7.5 trillion and states will spend $2.8 trillion on welfare, for a total of $10.3 trillion.

Washington can ill afford such expenditures. Uncle Sam ran more than $5 trillion in deficits over the past four years and is expected to run up a deficit of $845 billion this year. The Congressional Budget Office recently warned that while deficits are expected to decline over the next two years, they then will start rising again to $1 trillion annually. Over the next decade, assuming unrealistically that Congress doesn't add any new programs or increase outlays for any old ones, the accumulated red ink will be $7.0 trillion.

Welfare Programs Can Encourage Dependency on the Government

I think we should acknowledge that some welfare programs in the past were not well designed and in some cases did encourage dependency. As somebody who worked in low income neighborhoods, I've seen it where people weren't encouraged to work, weren't encouraged to upgrade their skills. They were just getting a check and over time their motivation started to diminish.

I will say that today welfare payments are not the big driver of our deficit or our debt. There are work obligations attached to welfare that the vast majority of folks who are getting welfare, want to work but can't find jobs. And what we should be doing in all our social programs is upgrading people's skills, giving them the tools they need to get into the workforce, nudging them into the workforce, but letting them know that we are there to encourage you and support you as long as you're showing the kind of responsibility for being willing to work that every American should be expected to show.

"Transcript: President Obama's Twitter Town Hall,"
Newsmax, *July 7, 2011. www.newsmax.com.*

Alas, this is merely the brief break before the tsunami of entitlement outlays hits. The total unfunded liability for Social Security and Medicare exceeds $100 trillion. To that must be added a long list of contingent, likely, and potential liabilities. Even the Post Office is broke and needs a bail-out! Economist Laurence Kotlikoff estimated total federal indebtedness at an astonishing $222 trillion.

Despite facing financial doom, government provides welfare to "a growing number of people who increasingly are not 'needy' by any rational definition," write Carleson and Mashburn. Wasteful duplication isn't limited to welfare, of course. Yet abuse of programs supposedly directed at human needs seems especially odious. There are people in need. In their name government is taxing away people's earnings and wasting the proceeds.

It's important not to focus solely on money. If the programs worked the amount being spent might not seem so excessive. However, observed Tanner, last year the nearly $1 trillion spent on welfare amounted "to $20,610 for every poor person in America, or $61,830 per poor family of three." With that kind of spending, no one should still be poor.

Yet when testifying before Congress in 2011, Patricia Dalton of the General Accountability Office refused to "hazard a guess" as to what percentage of federal welfare programs achieved their objectives. She admitted that it "would be good to have a number of how many programs there are, what exactly are we spending, and what are we getting for that money." Yes, that would be good.

Unfortunately, over the years it became increasingly evident that welfare did much to discourage marriage and work, and destroy family and community. That is, behavioral poverty accompanied material poverty. The result, complained the Heritage Foundation's Robert Rector and Jennifer Marshall, "has been the disintegration of the work ethic, family structure, and social fabric of large segments of the American population, which has in turn created a new dependency class." This directly threatens the American vision of self-government by independent citizens.

Yet the system is tenaciously defended by all of the usual interest groups which benefit from extensive federal wealth transfers. President Reagan argued that "The war on poverty created a great new upper-middle class of bureaucrats that found they had a fine career as long as they could keep enough needy people there to justify their existence." Officials may not exactly scheme to prevent the poor from leaving welfare. But welfare gives many people an interest in preserving existing programs.

One of Reagan's most notable achievements as two-term governor of California was confronting the seemingly unconstrained growth of welfare spending. Aided by Carleson, Gov. Reagan also opposed proposals by Presidents Lyndon Johnson and Richard Nixon for a guaranteed national income.

Reagan took center political stage when he was elected president in 1980. He brought Carleson to Washington and chose as his domestic policy adviser Hoover Institution scholar Martin Anderson, another trenchant critic of the Johnson-Nixon approach. Reagan made welfare reform one of his priorities, explaining: "States are better equipped than the federal government to administer effective welfare reforms if they are given broad authority to utilize administrative and policy discretion." However, the House remained in Democratic hands and welfare remained largely unchanged.

Still, the debate gradually shifted. Charles Murray's *Losing Ground: American Social Policy 1950–1980* crystallized the national realization that welfare wasted lives as well as money. When Republicans took control of both houses of Congress in 1994, welfare reform became a priority.

In 1996 President Bill Clinton signed legislation that turned Aid to Families with Dependent Children into Temporary Assistance to Needy Families. Federal matching grants became fixed block grants, with time limits and work requirements. The reform, explain Carleson and Mashburn, "reversed 61 years of U.S. welfare policy by ending a recipient's automatic entitlement to a cash welfare check. It was a good start, one on which Congress and the state legislatures can build a better future for millions of people still trapped by the incentives for dependency that remain in the remnants of the old welfare system."

It was a very good start. Millions of people were moved off welfare rolls into the workplace. Even many opponents of the legislation were forced to acknowledge the positive results. The good economy was important. But more important was the fact that recipients could no longer in effect marry welfare. TANF was determined to minimize both behavioral and material poverty.

However, the remnants that Carleson and Mashburn speak of remain a significant problem. As Elliott Gaiser recently observed in calling for further welfare reform, "the '96 welfare reform really only fixed one" program, AFDC. There are 156 to go! Moreover, the Democratic Congress and President Barack Obama together weakened the 1996 reforms, risking a slide back to a 1960s welfare dependency mentality. For instance, complain Carleson and Mashburn: "the Obama administration's policies have lured tens of millions of people onto the Food Stamp rolls, while loosening eligibility requirements for welfare programs across the board."

The way back won't be easy. America has spent decades creating the dependency-inducing welfare industry. The ultimate objective should be to reinforce and rebuild, when necessary, the traditional emphasis on personal, family, and community responsibility.

Indeed, this model of outward moving concentric rings of responsibility goes back to the Bible. Individuals were expected to work if possible, and not burden others. The Apostle Paul explained that a Christian who "failed to provide for his relatives, and especially his immediate family" was "worse than an unbeliever" (1 Timothy 5:8). The ancient Israelites and New Testament Christians alike created rules and procedures to aid those in need within their communities of faith. Finally, Paul wrote, "as we have opportunity, let us do good to all people" (Gal. 6:10).

Any government role should start only when private provision proves inadequate, and even then begin at the local and state levels. The national government should be the last, not first, resort. Even now we see some government efforts at reform, but primarily outside of Washington. For instance, Wisconsin Gov. Scott Walker plans to require work or job training to receive Food Stamps (now officially called the Supplemental Nutrition Assistance Program).

Carleson and Mashburn detail a state-based strategy in their new study, "Secure the Safety Net: Repeal and Replace the Welfare State." They look back past the 1996 reforms to Ronald Reagan's experience in California.

Welfare wasn't always viewed as Washington's job. Observe Carleson and Mashburn: "Welfare once was the province of the states, but increasingly has been treated as a federal responsibility. Since the 1960s, when the concept of public welfare radically expanded, federal micromanagement and redistribution of income has grown out of control." The most important first step that we could take is to push the welfare mass/mess back to the states.

Carleson and Mashburn propose eliminating 30 programs costing $849 million and consolidating into block grants another 127 programs costing $530 billion. More specifically, they would create seven block grants: community development, absorbing eight programs; cash assistance, replacing 11 programs; disability, transforming Supplemental Security Income for the Disabled; employment and training, consolidating 19 programs; housing, replacing 46 programs; medical assistance, incorporating 18 existing programs; and nutrition, consolidating 24 programs.

Equally important, the grants would be fixed, with a congressional vote required for any funding increase, and largely unrestricted, with federal oversight limited to audits of expenditures. Explain Carleson and Mashburn, transferring funds directly from the U.S. Treasury "would end federal, 'Washington-knows-best' bureaucratic interference and overreach. Governors would be able to design unified welfare systems tailored to best meet the needs of their low-income citizens."

Obviously states are not perfect and their reputation suffered badly during the Civil Rights era. However, today states are by far more responsible, responsive, and innovative than the national government. The Great Society needs to be replaced by the Free Society. Shifting power and responsibility out of Washington would begin what inevitably will be a lengthy and difficult process.

The current welfare system obviously is bad for taxpayers. It also is bad for poor people. Reform is desperately needed. Congress could begin the process tomorrow by turning national programs into state block grants. America can't afford to wait.

| "The trends of recent decades contrast sharply with the critics' assumption that social programs increasingly are supporting people who can work but choose not to do so."

Welfare Does Not Erode American Values

Arloc Sherman, Robert Greenstein, and Kathy Ruffing

In the following viewpoint, Arloc Sherman, Robert Greenstein, and Kathy Ruffing assert that contrary to critics' claims that government benefits are creating an entitlement society in which people depend on the government for their survival, the majority of people who benefit from these programs need the assistance they receive. The authors found in their analysis that 91 percent of the benefits go to elderly, disabled, or working households and that the middle class and poor receive their fair share of the benefits. They believe the data they collected effectively refutes the critics who bemoan the degeneration of US society into a welfare state as a result of government benefit programs. Sherman is a senior researcher at the Center on Budget and Policy Priorities

(CBPP) and author of the book Wasting America's Future. *Greenstein founded and serves as president of the CBPP. Ruffing is a senior fellow at the CBPP whose work focuses on the federal budget.*

As you read, consider the following questions:

1. Of the 9 percent of government benefit recipients who are not elderly or disabled, for what four purposes do 7 percent of these individuals receive benefits, as stated by the authors?

2. According to the results of the authors' study, what was the middle class's share of entitlement benefits compared to their size?

3. How did the benefits shares break down based on race with regard to non-Hispanic whites and Hispanics, as found in the study?

Some conservative critics of federal social programs, including leading presidential candidates, are sounding an alarm that the United States is rapidly becoming an "entitlement society" in which social programs are undermining the work ethic and creating a large class of Americans who prefer to depend on government benefits rather than work. A new CBPP [Center on Budget and Policy Priorities] analysis of budget and Census data, however, shows that *more than 90 percent of the benefit dollars that entitlement and other mandatory programs spend go to assist people who are elderly, seriously disabled, or members of working households*—not to able-bodied, working-age Americans who choose not to work. This figure has changed little in the past few years.

In a December 2011 op-ed, former Massachusetts Governor Mitt Romney warned ominously of the dangers that the nation faces from the encroachment of the "Entitlement Society," predicting that in a few years, "we will have created a society that contains a sizable contingent of long-term jobless, dependent on government benefits for survival." "Government dependency," he wrote, "can only foster passivity and sloth." Similarly, former Senator Rick Santorum said that recent expansions in the "reach of government" and the spending behind them are "systematically destroying the work ethic."

The claim behind these critiques is clear: federal spending on entitlements and other mandatory programs through which individuals receive benefits is promoting laziness, creating a dependent class of Americans who are losing the desire to work and would rather collect government benefits than find a job.

Most Social Programs Benefit the Elderly and Disabled

Such beliefs are starkly at odds with the basic facts regarding social programs, the analysis finds. Federal budget and Census data show that, in 2010, 91 percent of the benefit dollars from entitlement and other mandatory programs went to the elderly (people 65 and over), the seriously disabled, and members of working households. People who are neither elderly nor disabled—and do not live in a working household—received only 9 percent of the benefits.

Moreover, the vast bulk of that 9 percent goes for medical care, unemployment insurance [UI] benefits (which individuals must have a significant work history to receive), Social Security survivor benefits for the children and spouses of deceased workers, and Social Security benefits for retirees between ages 62 and 64. Seven out of the 9 percentage points go for one of these four purposes.

A small number of discretionary (i.e., non-entitlement) programs also provide substantial benefits to individuals, but the lack of full funding for some of these programs means they do not reach all eligible recipients. Indeed, in some cases—such as in low-income rental assistance programs—the vast *majority* of people who are eligible receive no benefits because of program funding limits. If we broaden the universe of programs examined to include the principal discretionary programs that provide benefits—low-income housing programs, the WIC nutrition program for low-income women and young children, and low-income energy assistance—the result is essentially unchanged. Some 90 percent of the benefit dollars still go to the elderly, the disabled, and working households.

This figure also changes little if we tweak the definition of a "working household" or of who is "disabled." This analysis defines a working household as one in which an individual works at least 1,000 hours in a year; raising the threshold to 1,500 hours makes little difference. This analysis defines a disabled person as one who receives Social Security disability benefits or the disability component of the Supplemental Security Income program (SSI) or who qualifies for Medicare on the basis of disability; modifying the definition to include disabled people who are not in one of these categories also makes little difference.

Moreover, if we look only at entitlement programs that are targeted to people with low incomes, the percentage of benefit dollars going to people who are elderly or disabled or members of working households remains high. Five of every six benefit dollars in these programs—83 percent—go to such people.

If anything, these figures *understate* the percentage of the benefits that generally go to people who are elderly, disabled, or members of working households. As noted, these data are for fiscal year 2010, a year when the unemployment rate averaged 9.6 percent and an unusually large number of Americans were in economic distress. In fiscal year 2007, the share of entitlement benefits going to people who are elderly or disabled or members of working households was a bit higher.

In short, both the current reality and the trends of recent decades contrast sharply with the critics' assumption that social programs increasingly are supporting people who can work but choose not to do so. In the 1980s and 1990s, the United States substantially reduced assistance to the jobless poor (through legislation such as the 1996 welfare law) while increasing assistance to low-income working families (such as through expansions of the Earned Income Tax Credit). The safety net became much more "work-based." In addition, the U.S. population is aging, which raises the share of benefits going to seniors and people with disabilities.

Most Populations Get Their Share of Benefits

The data in this analysis also dispel other common misperceptions, such as a belief (sometimes fanned by political figures) that entitlement programs shift substantial resources from the middle class to the poor. The data show that the middle class receives approximately its proportionate share of benefits: in 2010, the middle 60 percent of the population received 58 percent of the entitlement benefits. (The top 20 percent of the population received 10 percent of the benefits; the bottom 20 percent received 32 percent of the benefits.)

These figures contrast sharply with the distribution of the extensive deductions, credits, and other write-offs in the federal tax code, known as tax expenditures (former Federal Reserve Chair Alan Greenspan has called them "tax entitlements"). The Urban Institute-Brookings Institution Tax Policy Center estimates that for tax year 2011, the top fifth of the population will receive 66 percent of the $1.1 trillion in individual tax-expenditure benefits (the top 1 percent alone will receive 23.9 percent of the benefits), the middle 60 percent of the population will receive a little over 31 percent of the benefits, and the bottom 20 percent of the population will receive only 2.8 percent of the benefits.

Also, contrary to what a substantial share of Americans may assume, non-Hispanic whites receive slightly *more*, than their proportionate share of entitlement benefits. Non-Hispanic whites accounted for 64 percent of the population in 2010 and received 69 percent of the entitlement benefits. In contrast, Hispanics made up 16 percent of the population but received 12 percent of the benefits, less than their proportionate share—likely because they are a younger population and also because immigrants, including many legal immigrants, are ineligible for various benefits. Non-Hispanic African Americans account for 12 percent of the population and received 14 percent of the benefits.

Benefits Go to Those in Need

This analysis uses federal budget data on the benefit costs of various programs and Census data showing the percentage of the benefits in each program that go to different groups by age, employment, race, and other such factors. It covers all major entitlement programs *except* veterans' programs and military and civil service retirement, which critics presumably do not have in mind when they warn of the dangers of the "entitlement society" in fomenting dependency and sloth. But if we include veterans' and federal retirement programs, the share of benefits going to the elderly, the disabled, and working households remains unchanged at 91 percent.

The entitlement and mandatory programs covered in the analysis are Social Security, Medicare, Medicaid, unemployment insurance, SNAP (formerly known as the Food Stamp Program), SSI, Temporary Assistance for Needy Families (TANF), the school lunch program, the Children's Health Insurance Program (CHIP), the Earned Income Tax Credit, and the refundable component of the Child Tax Credit. This is the full list of entitlement or mandatory programs (other than the veterans' and federal retirement programs) for which the Census Bureau collects data on which beneficiaries receive them. It includes every entitlement or mandatory benefit program with annual federal and state expenditures of over $10 billion other than veterans' and federal retirement programs.

These programs accounted for $1.8 trillion in federal expenditures in 2010 out of a total of $2.1 trillion in entitlement and mandatory program costs; most of the remaining amount goes for the veterans' and federal retirement programs. We also include in this analysis $130 billion in *state* funding for benefits in the three programs that operate as federal-state partnerships: Medicaid, TANF, and CHIP.

We examined as well a somewhat broader group of programs that includes the same entitlement and mandatory programs but adds low-income housing programs, WIC, and LIHEAP [Low-Income Home Energy Assistance Program]—the largest discretionary programs that provide benefits, other than Pell Grants (for which reliable Census data on recipients are not available).

All Findings Confirm the Need of Benefits for Recipients

- In 2010, 91 percent of the benefits provided through entitlement programs went to people who were elderly (65 or older), disabled (receiving Social Security disability benefits, SSI disability benefits, or Medicare on the basis of a disability—all three programs use essentially the same disability standard, which limits eligibility to people with medically certified disabilities that leave them substantially unable to work), or members of a household in which an individual worked at least 1,000 hours during the year. As noted, the 91 percent figure is unchanged if one includes veterans' and federal retirement programs.

- This analysis defines working households as those in which someone has worked at least 1,000 hours a year. This is a conservative definition. If two household members work more than 1,000 hours between them

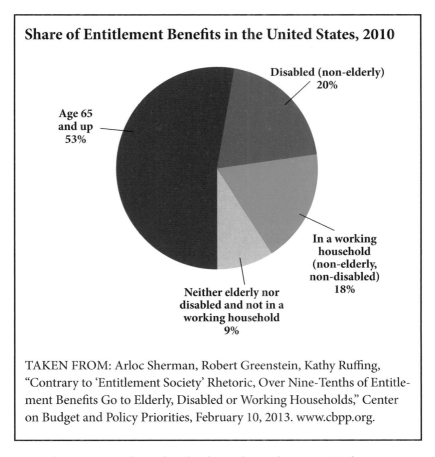

Share of Entitlement Benefits in the United States, 2010

Disabled (non-elderly)
20%

Age 65
and up
53%

In a working
household
(non-elderly,
non-disabled)
18%

Neither elderly nor
disabled and not in a
working household
9%

TAKEN FROM: Arloc Sherman, Robert Greenstein, Kathy Ruffing, "Contrary to 'Entitlement Society' Rhetoric, Over Nine-Tenths of Entitlement Benefits Go to Elderly, Disabled or Working Households," Center on Budget and Policy Priorities, February 10, 2013. www.cbpp.org.

but no single individual works at least 1,000 hours, we do not classify the unit as a working household.

- We also do not count people receiving unemployment insurance benefits as workers, although such individuals must have amassed a significant work record to qualify for UI. If we include people receiving UI as workers—in other words, if we ask what share of entitlement benefits go to people who are elderly or disabled or receive UI, or are members of households in which an individual works at least 1,000 hours—the share rises from 91 percent to 94 percent. The percentage edges down to 92 percent if we count UI recipients but raise the "hours-of-work threshold" from 1,000 hours

of work to 1,500 hours. If we define working households as those in which an individual worked at least
1,500 hours but do not count UI beneficiaries as workers, the percentage declines slightly to 88 percent.

- If we add in the principal discretionary programs that
help people meet basic needs (low-income housing,
WIC, and LIHEAP) and examine both them and the
entitlement and other mandatory programs, the 91 percent figure drops to 90 percent.

- This analysis uses a narrow definition of disability that
misses individuals who become disabled so young that
they haven't amassed enough work history to qualify
for Social Security Disability Insurance or Medicare,
and whose countable household income or assets are
over the very low SSI eligibility limits, which are below
the poverty line. If we broaden the definition to include
other adults who report work-limiting disabilities in the
Census survey data, the percentage of benefits going to
people who are elderly or disabled or members of
working households rises from 91 percent to 92 percent.

- If we look only at *means-tested* entitlement and other
mandatory programs—that is, programs limited to low-
income people—the percentage of benefits going to the
elderly, the disabled, or working households remains
high at 83 percent, a robust percentage for programs
that are limited to people with low incomes. This high
percentage reflects policy changes in recent decades that
have substantially restricted benefits for poor people
who lack earnings (other than the elderly and
disabled), while increasing assistance for low-income
working families with children, especially in the form
of tax credits. The 83 percent figure edges down to 82
percent if low-income housing programs, WIC, and
LIHEAP are included.

- More than half (53 percent) of entitlement benefits go to seniors. Some 73 percent of the benefits go to people who are elderly or disabled; most of the rest goes to working households.

- The data contradict beliefs that entitlements take heavily from the middle class to give to people at the bottom or that they shower benefits on the very wealthy. The middle 60 percent of the population receives close to 60 percent of the benefits. The top 5 percent of the population receives about 3 percent of the benefits.

Tweaking the Data Does Not Significantly Impact the Results

This analysis describes who receives government benefits. To estimate where government benefit dollars go, we use Census Bureau data to calculate the percentage of these benefits received by particular groups, and apply those percentages to budget totals for each program from administrative data from the Office of Management and Budget or program records.

The analysis is limited to assistance in programs for which data are available from our main Census Bureau source, the Annual Social and Economic Supplement of the Current Population Survey (CPS), commonly called the March CPS. Our 2010 figures use the March 2011 CPS, which asks about calendar year 2010 income.

People who live in institutions present a special case. Some 17.6 percent of Medicaid benefits and about 5.2 percent of Medicare benefits go to people in nursing homes and other institutional settings. The CPS is a *household* survey and does not include people who live in institutions. However, the Census Bureau's American Community Survey [ACS] does cover those individuals. Accordingly, we use ACS data to distribute Medicaid and Medicare benefits that go to people living in institutions. (For other benefits we examine, the share going to people in institutions is generally very small or non-existent, and we do not make a similar adjustment.)

This analysis includes spending for benefits (assistance to individuals); it excludes program expenditures that do not go for benefits—primarily administrative costs. *State* funding is included in jointly run federal-state programs that require state matching funds—Medicaid, the Children's Health Insurance Program (CHIP), and Temporary Assistance for Needy Families (TANF). Payments to beneficiaries living in U.S. territories or other countries (such as a Social Security retiree living abroad) are excluded because overseas data are not available from the CPS.

We examine Census data on the age, disability status, and race of the individuals who receive the assistance, and the number of hours worked by the household member with the most work hours. Annual work hours are estimated by multiplying the number of weeks worked by the usual number of work hours per week.

Wherever possible, we distribute dollars, not persons. For example, rather than looking at the percentage of Social Security recipients who are 65 and older, we look at the percentage of Social Security dollars that go to recipients 65 and older.

For some programs, the Census Bureau does not ask survey respondents about the dollar value of benefits received but Census estimates the dollar value based on a combination of other available survey data and program data. For example, while Census asks respondents about whether they receive housing assistance, it does not ask about the value of rental assistance received; however, the Bureau calculates the value of the rent subsidy using other data including annual household cash income, the size and composition of the household, local fair market rent levels, and program rules. We use these Census estimates of the amount of housing assistance that various households receive, as well as similar Census estimates for the value of school lunch and WIC benefits. For the value of tax credits, we use estimated credits available on the CPS file, which Census calculates based on the family's reported income, earnings, and composition, as well as on national tax statistics from the IRS.

In cases where Census has data on who receives a benefit but has not estimated the dollar value of the benefit—specifically, for Medicare and Medicaid recipients in institutions—we allocate total benefit dollars from program records using the Census data on the distribution of program recipients rather than program dollars. This effectively assumes that benefits have the same average value across the institutionalized population.

In general, we use individual income values in the Census data, assigning all Social Security benefits, for example, to the specific individual or individuals within the household who report receiving that income. In the case of benefits such as housing assistance, SNAP, and home energy assistance that generally go to an entire *household* rather than to individuals, we assign each household member their per-person share of the benefit. Likewise, in the case of benefits that typically support *families* (such as TANF), we allocate the per-person value of the benefit equally across all members of the family.

Confirming the Need of Recipients

We define old age and disability at the individual level. For example, if a family of two contains a 65-year-old Social Security recipient and his or her 64-year-old spouse who also receives Social Security as an early retiree, we count only the 65-year-old individual's benefit as going to a person who is elderly. (In our core analysis, disability refers to reported receipt of Social Security disability benefits, SSI, or Medicare among those younger than 65.)

We define work at the household level. Thus, if a household contains a child, an individual who worked substantially through the year, and that individual's unemployed spouse, the benefits going to all household members are counted as going to a working household.

When we examine benefits by income, we sort the population into income groups based on household cash income adjusted for household size, using the same method that CBO [the Congressional Budget Office] uses to examine income and benefit receipt and tax burdens by income group. Like CBO, when we group individuals into fifths by household income, each fifth contains the same number of persons (not households).

Limitations of the Study Do Not Undermine the Results

Our Census data have several limitations. For example, the CPS likely misses most benefits paid to individuals who died between the calendar year (2010) and the survey month (generally March of the following year); this omission may bias our results toward younger recipients. Conversely, benefits paid to someone who was 64 years old in 2010 but turned 65 early the next year before the March 2011 CPS may be classified as going to someone age 65. Also, as previously noted, the CPS leaves out the institutionalized population; while our analysis includes the dollars going to people in institutions, we lack complete data on how these dollars are distributed. Total spending levels from program records are for the fiscal year, while the Census data used to distribute them are for the calendar year.

Another limitation is under-reporting. In the CPS and ACS, as in most surveys, respondents may forget or omit some of their income. Moreover, some benefits tend to be under-reported more than others. We deal with this data limitation by using Census data only to estimate the percentage distribution of each program's benefits; we apply that distribution to the *actual spending totals* for each program as shown in official budget and program records. This eliminates any bias due to differences in under-reporting between programs. (If we had used pure Census data, our figures would show that 92 percent, rather than 91 percent, of entitlement and other mandatory benefit spending in 2010 went to seniors, people with disabilities, and working households.) It is still possible for some bias to exist due to variations in the amount of under-reporting between different types of recipients within a program.

> *"While the term 'breadwinner' conjures up images of pleasingly plump paychecks, the real story here is the rise of poor single mothers."*

An Increase in the Number of Female Breadwinners Threatens American Traditions

Selwyn Duke

In the following viewpoint, Selwyn Duke makes the claim that the rise in female breadwinners in the United States does not mean that women are getting ahead but rather that men are making less, or worse, making no financial contribution to the family. Duke cites that in the 1940s, the percentage of single mother families was around 4 percent compared to 41 percent today. He explains that this is bad for the United States because there has never been a successful society where women are head of the household. He asserts that this is because societies work best when the male is the money earner and the female raises the children. He believes that without this system, children are more likely to grow up lacking guidance and strong morals. Duke is a writer, columnist, and public speaker whose work has been published widely online and in print.

As you read, consider the following questions:

1. According to the author, of the 40 percent of women breadwinners, what percent of them are single mothers?

2. Why, in the author's view, is a wage gap between men and women in the United States not a bad thing?

3. The author says that a female-led household is not good for society; what reasons does he give?

When women start doing what men have traditionally done, yours is a civilization of the setting sun. This is brought to mind when pondering a recent [May 2013] Pew Research Center study showing that women are now the primary or sole breadwinners in 40 percent of American households. You may have heard the story—it created quite a stir on Fox News, with Greta Van Susteren and Megyn Kelly (who became quite hysterical) taking exception to male colleagues' warnings about the development's sociological implications. But if these two ladies, and the other critics, had reacted rationally and not emotionally, they would realize what is obvious:

The rise in female breadwinners is a sign of a civilization in decline.

More Female Breadwinners Really Means More Single Mothers

Let's start by first examining the study. While the term "breadwinner" conjures up images of pleasingly plump paychecks, the real story here is the rise of poor single mothers. Among the 40 percent of women in the breadwinner group, *63 percent* are single mothers. This isn't surprising, since the rate of single motherhood has risen from about 4 percent in the 1940s to 41 percent today (72 percent in the black community). So what kind of "bread" are we talking about? Writes Amy Langfield of CNBC, "The median income for a single mother who has never been married was $17,400 as of

2011." And, obviously, having large numbers of single mothers, with essentially fatherless children, struggling to make ends meet isn't good for the women, the children, or the society as a whole.

The picture looks better for the married 37 percent of the breadwinner group, but only by comparison. Twenty-nine percent of these women's husbands are unemployed. Moreover, Pew describes these women as older, college-educated, and white. Translation: they're the one-child wonders. These are often women who postpone childbirth in deference to careerism and then, perhaps after dropping a tidy sum at a fertility clinic, have their sole son or daughter. Why does this warrant mention? Because as the documentary *Demographic Winter* points out, this phenomenon is a significant contributing factor to the plummeting birth rates among Western peoples. Outside New Zealand, there isn't one major European-descent group with a replacement-level birth rate. And for all you secular-feminist chauvinists so proud of your cultural hegemony, what do you think happens to values that cause people to erase themselves?

So why can't the Megyn Kellys of the world perceive the rise in female breadwinners as the warning sign it is? Because their feminist dogma teaches that any female "gain" relative to men is positive, and any criticism of it is blind male chauvinism. These are the people who cheer girls' "better" performance in schools even though this is largely attributable to boys' worsening performance (and improved female test scores aren't relevant, because the exams, like the boys, have been dumbed down). It's a mindset that would consider it a good thing if women won every future marathon because men either lost their legs or stopped running.

And that is the point. If a warring nation must move a few divisions from the southern front to shore up the northern, it isn't a victory for those divisions; it means the war effort is waning. And if the divisions' generals view it as a per-

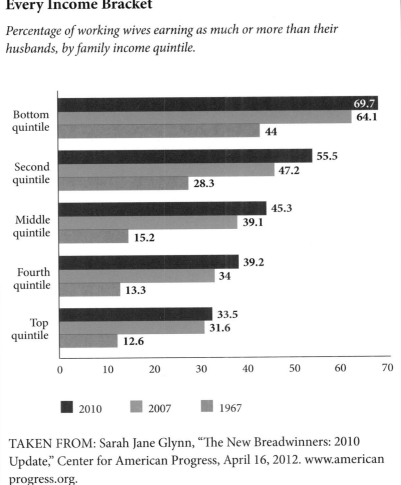

The Number of Women Breadwinners Has Increased in Every Income Bracket

Percentage of working wives earning as much or more than their husbands, by family income quintile.

Income quintile	2010	2007	1967
Bottom quintile	69.7	64.1	44
Second quintile	55.5	47.2	28.3
Middle quintile	45.3	39.1	15.2
Fourth quintile	39.2	34	13.3
Top quintile	33.5	31.6	12.6

■ 2010   ■ 2007   ■ 1967

TAKEN FROM: Sarah Jane Glynn, "The New Breadwinners: 2010 Update," Center for American Progress, April 16, 2012. www.american progress.org.

sonal victory because they'll have the opportunity to distinguish themselves, they're self-centered and ignorant.

Female-Led Households Are Bad for Society

Likewise, it was a sign of crisis when women had to assume men's roles in the factories during WWII, but the idea was that the crisis would end and normalcy resume. But today we are in perpetual war—culture war—in a never-ending crisis in which we fight ourselves and confuse losses with gains. No, the intersex wage gap isn't a bad thing, and it isn't good when it starts to close. The size of that gap correlates with the health of the nuclear family; the larger it is, the greater men's ability to support their families and women's opportunity to stay at home with the children. No, it isn't good when girls outshine boys in school, as this reflects a society of undisciplined lads and a hostile yet permissive, feminist-oriented academia.

And, no, it isn't good when you destroy patriarchy. Why? G.K. Chesterton [English writer and philosopher] put it best when he wrote, "What is called matriarchy is simply moral anarchy, in which the mother alone remains fixed because all the fathers are fugitive and irresponsible." If you want matriarchy, just go into the black community. Women rule the roost there, but they reign in a hell born of degraded morals and family breakdown. There has never been a successful matriarchy—the notion of a matriarchal prehistory is a myth—and there never will be.

This is why, ultimately, the feminist model is destined for the dustbin of history. The only system that ensures the perpetuation of civilization (replacement-level birth rates) is patriarchy; the only system that compels women *and* men to fulfill their responsibilities to hearth and home is patriarchy. And this is why, barring the end of man or a dystopian future in which children are lab-created assembly-line style to be the collective's drones, patriarchy is inevitable.

There is no substitute for tradition. The Soviets learned this the hard way, for after undermining the family, sex roles, and religion, mass murderer Joseph Stalin [the Russian Socialist dictator] actually outlawed abortion in a vain attempt to combat a bottomed-out birth rate. But today Russia's population is still declining by 700,000 per year—the wages of their statist sin.

When a people would be invaded or conquered years ago, the men and boys above a certain age would sometimes be killed. Emasculate a society, and it's no longer a force to be reckoned with. But we have emasculated ourselves, killing off manhood by neutering men emotionally, intellectually, and spiritually. This won't end well, but for sure it will end. Because the feminist band can play on, but the rising water will soon drown out their music—for good.

| "*Human hunter-gatherers don't partici-pate in modern economies.*"

Women Breadwinners: The Natural Order

The Economist

In the following viewpoint, The Economist argues that the rise in female breadwinners in the United States is positive for the country, and arguments to the contrary are alarmist and sexist. The author takes issue with the opposing argument that the rise in women earners signifies an increase in poor single mothers and is bad for society, contending that studies have not shown whether households led by women have a positive or negative impact on society. The author points to statistics that suggest that the United States is becoming a safer and better country— implying that if the rise in female-led households were so damaging to society, more negative effects would be shown. The Economist *is a weekly newsmagazine.*

As you read, consider the following questions:

1. According to the Census Bureau data cited in the viewpoint, how many children live in a household in which the mother is the primary breadwinner?

2. What evidence does the author of this article use to support the claim that there is a wide variety of family types in nature?

3. What does the author identify as the "natural" role of men in modern society?

Census bureau data show that four in ten American children live in a household in which their mother is the primary breadwinner. In 1960 women brought home most of the bacon in just 11% of households with kids. Another benchmark in the grinding struggle for women's equality? Not according to the indignant panelists in this glorious Fox Business segment, led by the professionally choleric Lou Dobbs [TV personality and radio host].

Juan Williams [Fox News contributor] fears the worst. In the rise of lady-led households, Mr Williams says, "you're seeing the disintegration of marriage. . . . You're seeing, I think, systemically . . . something going terribly wrong in American society, and it's hurting our children. And it's going to have impact for generations to come. Left, right—I don't see how you can argue this!" I suggest empiricism. Elspeth Reeve of the *Atlantic* digs up a few facts:

> What is going terribly wrong in American society? Crime rates are at historic lows. So are teen pregnancy rates. Worker productivity is high. Dobbs mentioned the high dropout rate, but it's declined from 12.1 percent in 1990 to 7.4 percent in 2010. He said we needed to "teach our kids to read and write," but the literacy rate is 99 percent. Very few people even smoke anymore. America is kind of awesome, actually, despite all these terrible working women.

Mr Williams's co-panelist, Erick Erickson, a fellow advocate of the scientific method, condemns the trend on biological grounds:

Both Women's and Men's Roles Have Changed

Between 1965 and 2000, the number of working mothers in the United States rose from 45 to 78 percent of all mothers, and the average time that an American woman spent in the paid labor force increased from 9 to 25 hours a week. Yet women were still devoting nearly 40 hours a week to family care: housework, child care, shopping. Men, by contrast, spent only 21, most of which were devoted to fairly discrete and flexible tasks like mowing the lawn, washing the car, and tossing softballs with the kids. . . .

Yes, women incontrovertibly do more work around the home. But men, to be fair, have also leapt pretty dramatically into a rapidly evolving rearrangement of roles. Between 1965 and 1983, married fathers more than doubled their housework hours, from four hours per week to 10. They tripled their time spent on primary child care between 1965 and 2000, from two and a half hours per week to nearly eight. These men may do the household chores differently than their wives would.

Debora Spar, Daily Beast,
September 24, 2012. www.thedailybeast.com.

I'm so used to liberals telling conservatives that they're antiscience. But liberals who defend this and say it is not a bad thing are very anti-science. When you look at biology—when you look at the natural world—the roles of a male and a female in society and in other animals, the male typically is the dominant role. The female, it's not antithesis, or it's not competing, it's a complementary role.

One admires at least the aspiration to science.

Not All Species Are Ruled by Males

There is, in fact, stupefying variety in the animal kingdom, so it's hard to say what is typical. The species genetically closest to our own are bonobos and chimpanzees. Chimps are an aggressive, "male dominant" species, but peaceable bonobos dwell in female dominant groups, in which the females, tightly bonded through frequent mutual masturbation, gang up to suppress and subdue male aggression. Bonobos surely find the non-genital nature of ritualised human greeting bizarrely cold, if not outright unnatural. I doubt Mr Erickson wishes to suggest that this somehow implies that human advocates of the handshake, curtsy, or bow are "anti-science". Moreover, whether we look to chimps or our sexy bonobo cousins, it's challenging to identify anything resembling the Census Bureau's notion of a "household", nor is it easy to come by income data for chimp and bonobo labour-market participants. Perhaps this has something to do with the fact that non-human primates do not, as far as we know, function within an extended market order characterised by a refined division of labour and the exchange of money for goods and services.

Actually, human hunter-gatherers don't participate in modern economies, either, so it's hard to know how to use even the primeval behaviour of our own species as a norm for evaluating the alarming trend in the earning power of moms. In any case, my understanding of the relevant bits of anthropology is that hunter-gatherer women generally specialise in reliable food-gathering, while men generally specialise in unreliable hunting, and it is by no means unusual for women to contribute more than men to their group's caloric budget. According to one theory, hunting gives men an opportunity to display their genetic mettle, so they do it to attract mates as much as to bring home the wild-boar bacon. What's natural to men is not a "dominant" economic role within the modern, nuclear family unit, but a habit of posturing—often wastefully, often pathetically—meant to secure social status and impress women. In this sense, Lou Dobbs and his guests defend through their manner more than their words the prerogatives of men.

Humans Have Come a Long Way

On Wednesday [May 29, 2013], I speculated about the sometimes fanciful liberal tendency to see themselves as drum majors of history. Mr Erickson's appeal to the natural order points to a matched conservative folly: the tendency to imagine the familiar, recent past in especial accord with timeless human nature. Once one considers how far we've come since the Pleistocene—what with all our capitalism, nation-states, dentistry and cable news—this sort of biological essentialism seems unbecoming of conservatives who, if they are about anything worthwhile, are about the defence and advancement of civilisation. The defence of atavistic privilege, which invariably proceeds on the basis of specious claims about natural hierarchy, is the hardy, incivil part of conservatism. Gentlepersons left and right will leave this nastiness behind, and cheer the ongoing economic achievements of the fairer and not-yet-equal sex.

Periodical and Internet Sources Bibliography

The following articles have been selected to supplement the diverse views presented in this chapter.

Julia Baird	"Seeking a Moral Compass," *Newsweek*, February 22, 2010.
Jeremy Black	"Big Government: Good and Bad," *New Criterion*, January 2010.
Robert J. Bresler	"The Economy's Cultural Crisis," *USA Today Magazine*, March 2009.
Daniel Callahan	"America's Blind Spot," *Commonweal*, October 9, 2009.
Gary Dorrien	"No Common Good?," *Christian Century*, April 19, 2011.
Steve Forbes	"What Obama Doesn't Get About the U.S.," *Forbes*, November 5, 2012.
Harriet Fraad	"American Depressions," *Tikkun*, January/February 2010.
Paul Ryan	"Debt Crisis Is a Threat to Our Way of Life!" *Veterans' Vision*, 2010.
Jacob Weisberg	"The Staying Power of the S Word," *Newsweek*, March 16, 2009.
Kenneth D. Whitehead	"Feint of Heart," *Touchstone: A Journal of Mere Christianity*, July/August 2013.

OPPOSING
VIEWPOINTS®
SERIES

CHAPTER 3

Should Americans Promote Patriotism?

Chapter Preface

According to an April 2013 Gallup poll, 45 percent of Americans surveyed indicated that they had exerted a "special effort" to buy American-made products over the past year. Of those who had "bought American," 32 percent stated that their motivation was to be patriotic and support the nation; 31 percent maintained that they were driven to purchase American-made goods to keep jobs in the country; and 20 percent acknowledged the act was good for the country's economy in general. Few of those polled were concerned with the quality of foreign goods or operated under the belief that US products were superior to their overseas counterparts. Still, 64 percent—most of whom were older than thirty years old—said they would be willing to pay more for goods that were made in the United States.

In a April 30 Gallup briefing, Jeffrey M. Jones claimed, "Patriotism and concern for the health of the U.S. economy are major reasons behind people's shopping for American-made products, but those attributes may be in shorter supply among younger Americans who find less appeal in U.S.-made goods. In fact, Gallup has found younger people in the U.S. ranking among the least patriotic subgroups of Americans." Polls, however, do not convey the opinions of those who decry the perceived loss of patriotism among the nation's youth. In a July 2012 article for *PN*, a publication of the Paralyzed Veterans of America, editor Richard Hoover writes about "the lack of recognition by our young people of the sacrifices that have been made for them." In Hoover's view, most young people have failed to grasp the value of patriotism because the nation has turned away from it. For instance, he states that many Americans—but particularly the young—have no measurable stake in the current military engagements in the Middle East because they have not been called upon to serve.

To him, patriotism might return if all Americans were compelled to perform military or civic service to show their devotion to the country and its principles.

On December 24, 2001, *US News & World Report* editor at large and political analyst David Gergen posed similar ideas in the shadow of the tragic events of September 11. He added, "A culture of service might also help reverse the trend among many young people to shun politics and public affairs." However, according to Gergen, the terrorist attacks of that year touched the patriotic zeal dormant in many young people, but the lack of a national plan to capitalize on that patriotism and provide outlets for it left the feeling stillborn. Roughly two months after Gergen's report, Harvard assistant professor and liberal pollster Anna Greenberg echoed these thoughts by blaming the death of patriotism among young Americans on disenchantment with big government's ability to instill trust and direction. "Both Generations X and Y were raised without national political leadership that clearly articulated a vision of government's role in creating a better society," she wrote in a February 11, 2002, article for *The Nation*. As Greenberg explains, the country's youth were open to patriotic action in the wake of 9/11, "but transforming this attention and energy into something politically tangible requires leadership." Instead Greenberg points out the leadership told all Americans that the best thing they could do in response to the terrorist attacks was to go back to work and continue their lives as they had before—seemingly endorsing a kind of amnesia instead of provoking young people to act.

Views on the place of patriotism in the post-9/11 world are still part of a national debate, as the viewpoints in the following chapter illustrate. Authors contest the meaning and value of patriotism in the twenty-first-century United States and the manner in which it should or should not be aligned with the fundamental values of the nation.

> *"Patriotism represents a loyalty not to land or national borders but instead a steadfast adherence to a set of principles that are greater than an individual person."*

Americans Should Embrace Patriotism

Jose Cespedes

In the following viewpoint, Jose Cespedes contends that American patriotism means more than just beating the drum for a person's particular country. He argues that American patriotism is different because the United States represents commitment to an ideal not just a land. Cespedes explains that American values come from a belief that every person has certain rights as a human being, and the US Constitution protects those rights. To be patriotic, in his opinion, is to support those human rights. Cespedes claims that the Left is seen as unpatriotic because they blame the United States for problems in the world instead of seeing the nation as a force of good; the author believes this view contradicts the beliefs of most Americans. Cespedes majored in history and government at Bowdoin College. He wrote the "Country First" column in the Bowdoin Orient.

As you read, consider the following questions:

1. In this viewpoint Cespedes says that fundamental American rights, such as freedom of speech and democratic elections, were developed over time by whom?

2. According to the author, what does it mean to be American?

3. Cespedes believes most Americans see the US position in the world how?

Patriotism, defined as a dedication to one's country and loyalty to the principles for which it stands, vastly transcends most other manifestations of pride.

Pride in a local sports team, alma mater, or even occupation may mean a great deal to an individual, but it is ultimately the bond between a person and his or her country that the most has been sacrificed for, both in terms of cost and life.

The rank and file of the intellectual left is no doubt puzzled by such a dynamic. There is no logic, their argument goes, in killing and dying for a country that you were merely born into.

For these individuals, a country is little more than a piece of land and to tether one's identity and livelihood with it is purely nonsensical.

What the perpetrators of such misconceptions fail to fully realize, however, is that patriotism is man's way of adhering to and defending values larger then himself and his narrow sphere of influence.

Patriotism represents a loyalty not to land or national borders but instead a steadfast adherence to a set of principles that are greater than an individual person.

Recently, some have tried to claim that values and human rights can be divorced from one another, that in some blatantly biased representation of the political right, conservatives

How Proud Are You to Be an American?

	Extremely proud	Very proud	Less proud*
By race			
White, non Hispanic	52%	31%	14%
Black, non Hispanic	36%	45%	17%
By age group			
18–29	39%	32%	27%
30–49 53%	30%	13%	
50–64	60%	30%	9%
65 and over	55%	31%	12%
By political party			
Republican	69%	24%	5%
Democratic	43%	40%	15%
Independent	53%	29%	17%
All respondents	52%	31%	14%

* Includes those saying moderately/only a little bit/not at all proud.

Data from Pew Research Center, June 24–27, 2010 survey. Figures may not add up to 100 because of rounding

TAKEN FROM: Pew Research Center, "Proud Patriots—and Harsh Critics of Government," July 1, 2010. www.pewresearch.org.

seek to perpetuate a value system that excludes many, while the left somehow nobly defends essential human rights.

Yet in the rush to portray the conservative right maliciously, the indelible influence values have on our conception of human rights is tossed aside.

American Patriotism Shows a Belief in Fundamental Human Rights

The harsh reality, at least for the left, is that what Americans uphold as fundamental human rights, such as free speech, habeas corpus [the right to a trial], democratic elections and so on, stem from a distinctly western value system that was developed over time by political theorists.

Part of what fuels the concept of American exceptionalism is the recognition that prior to the founding, the idea of a modern democratic-republic that afforded its citizens such rights was seen as outlandish and purely theoretical.

It was a willingness to believe that such rights were essential and fundamental to the human condition, in essence an adherence to the rightness of a particular value system over any other, that enabled men like [Founding Fathers Thomas] Jefferson and [James] Madison to shape the core documents of our nation.

All this is by way of explaining that what we understand as human rights, as Americans, is shaped profoundly by our communal values. We can no more separate the two concepts than we can the moon from the stars.

To be sure, values can and do change over time, but others are fixed and essential. To be American means having a willingness to adhere to the rule of law, to position democracy as the best form of government and to revere the principles enshrined in our Constitution.

To be a proud American is to recognize, embrace and uphold the belief that such values are distinctly American. Whatever status these values hold in the world now as fundamental human rights, it is because of the sacrifices made by generations of Americans to privilege them above competing notions about the human experience.

Where would democracy and the rights enshrined in the Constitution be without the United States as force to uphold them in the world?

When [President] John F. Kennedy said in his inaugural address, "Let every nation know . . . that we shall pay any price, bear any burden, meet any hardship, support any friend, oppose any foe, in order to assure the survival and the success of liberty," he was underscoring a national commitment to very particular values.

The belief that these values and our notion of human rights could be seen as one and the same speaks to the success of the American experiment with democracy. And yes, despite the anti-American vitriol so sadly typical in left-wing dogma, that is an achievement all Americans can be proud of.

Given all this, then, it comes as little surprise that for so many generations of Americans, the left's argument that "dissent is patriotic" rings hollow. While dissent may not necessarily be unpatriotic, the claim that a refutation of American values and principles is indeed patriotic wholly ignores what American patriotism means in the first place.

The willingness of an individual to identify with American values and embrace them, not reject them, is at the core of what American patriotism is about.

Slandering the modern Conservative movement (which, incidentally, has been defined by [political theorist] Russell Kirk, [conservative political commentator] Bill Buckley, [Senator] Barry Goldwater, [President] Ronald Reagan, etc. and not [first female governor of Alaska] Sarah Palin) as the reason why the left is viewed as unpatriotic is a tired, empty complaint.

Many Americans See the Left as Unpatriotic

If the left wants a reason for why so [many] Americans view them or their ideology as unpatriotic, they need to only read democrat Jeane Kirkpatrick's [US ambassador under Reagan] speech at the 1984 Republican National Convention.

Time and again, the left will find any way and any means to "blame America first" even when doing so is blatantly unfair.

The left's never-ending need to highlight what is wrong with America as opposed to celebrating what is right with it exemplifies the left's seeming contempt for the American dream and way of life.

To be sure, such a characterization of the left wing in American politics might indeed be unfair. Many leftists genuinely want to see the United States embrace a vision and value system in line with their own world view and there is nothing wrong with such a goal.

Most Americans, however, recognize America's position as a force for good in the world and are proud of it. They don't seek to change the American value system because they embrace it and see it as a part of themselves.

Rather than blame conservatives, if the left wants to change the public's perception of themselves as unpatriotic, they should first learn what American patriotism means in the first place.

I *"Love of country isn't natural. It's not something you're born with."*

Why I'm Not Patriotic

Matthew Rothschild

In the following viewpoint, Matthew Rothschild argues that he is antipatriotic both in general and toward the United States. In the general sense, the author critiques patriotism for being the root of many of the world's ills today and throughout history, calling up world wars and genocidal dictators as examples. With regard to the United States, Rothschild maintains that if Americans look honestly at the country's actions today, ranging from its foreign and domestic policies to its hegemonic strength, there are few reasons to be proud. Rothschild concludes that American patriotism should be abandoned to prevent further international atrocities and honestly address the problems within the country. Rothschild is a liberal journalist and commentator who has been the editor of The Progressive *magazine since 1994.*

As you read, consider the following questions:

1. What are three examples of the deadly consequences of nationalism throughout history given by the author?

2. Rothschild states that "love of country is a form of" what?

3. What are three questions that the author says he must ask when someone claims that the United States "is still the greatest country in the world"?

(In memory of George Carlin.)

It's July 4th again, a day of near-compulsory flag-waving and nation-worshipping. Count me out.

Spare me the puerile parades.

Don't play that martial music, white boy.

And don't befoul nature's sky with your F-16s.

You see, I don't believe in patriotism.

It's not that I'm anti-American, but I am anti-patriotic.

Love of country isn't natural. It's not something you're born with. It's an inculcated kind of love, something that is foisted upon you in the home, in the school, on TV, at church, during the football game.

Yet most people accept it without inspection.

Why?

For when you stop to think about it, patriotism (especially in its malignant morph, nationalism) has done more to stack the corpses millions high in the last 300 years than any other factor, including the prodigious slayer, religion.

The victims of colonialism, from the Congo to the Philippines, fell at nationalism's bayonet point.

World War I filled the graves with the most foolish nationalism. And Hitler and Mussolini and Imperial Japan brought nationalism to new nadirs. The flags next to the tombstones are but signed confessions—notes left by the killer after the fact.

The millions of victims of Stalin and Mao and Pol Pot have on their death certificates a dual diagnosis: yes communism, but also that other ism, nationalism.

The whole world almost got destroyed because of nationalism during the Cuban Missile Crisis.

The bloody battles in Serbia and Bosnia and Croatia in the 1990s fed off the injured pride of competing patriotisms and all their nourished grievances.

In the last five years in Iraq, tens of thousands or hundreds of thousands of Iraqi civilians have died because the United States, the patriarch of patriotism, saw fit to impose itself, without just cause, on another country. But the excuse was patriotism, wrapped in Bush's brand of messianic militarism: that we, the great Americans, have a duty to deliver "God's gift of freedom" to every corner of the world.

And the Congress swallowed it, and much of the American public swallowed it, because they've been fed a steady diet of this swill.

What is patriotism but "the narcissism of petty differences"? That's Freud's term, describing the disorder that compels one group to feel superior to another.

Then there's a little multiplication problem: Can every country be the greatest country in the world?

This belief system magically transforms an accident of birth into some kind of blue ribbon.

"It's a great country," said the old Quaker essayist Milton Mayer. "They're all great countries."

At times, the appeal to patriotism may be necessary, as when harnessing the group to protect against a larger threat (Hitler) or to overthrow an oppressor (as in the anti-colonial struggles in the Third World).

But it is always a dangerous toxin to play with, and it ought to be shelved with cross and bones on the label except in these most extreme circumstances.

In an article called "Patriot Games" in the current issue of *Time* magazine (July 7 [2008]), Peter Beinart, late of *The New Republic*, inspects his navel for seven pages and then throws the lint all around.

"Conservatives are right," he says. "To some degree, patriotism must mean loving your country for the same reason you love your family: simply because it is yours."

And then he criticizes, incoherently, the conservative love-it-or-leave-it types.

The moral folly of his argument he himself exposes: "If liberals love America purely because it embodies ideals like liberty, justice, and equality, why shouldn't they love Canada—which from a liberal perspective often goes further toward realizing those principles—even more? And what do liberals do," he asks, "when those universal ideals collide with America's self-interest? Giving away the federal budget to Africa would probably increase the net sum of justice and equality on the planet, after all. But it would harm Americans and thus be unpatriotic."

This is a straw man if I ever I saw one, but if the United States gave a lot more of its budget to eradicating poverty and disease in Africa and other parts of the developing world, it might actually make us all safer.

At bottom, note how readily Beinart disposes of "liberty, justice, and equality."

He has stripped patriotism to its vacuous essence: Love your country because it's yours.

If we stopped that arm from reflexively saluting and concerned ourselves more with "universal ideals" than with parochial ones, we'd be a lot better off.

We wouldn't be in Iraq, we wouldn't have besmirched ourselves at Guantanamo, we wouldn't be acting like some Argentinean junta that wages illegal wars and tortures people and disappears them into secret dungeons.

Love of country is a form of idolatry.

American Patriotism Destroys the "Hoop of Life"

American patriotic discourses regularly centre on inculcating in US citizens the belief that they are "the greatest nation on earth" and "the moral compass and beacon of hope for the rest of the world." I can assure you that, within the American empire, there are many, many cracks on the veneer of subject loyalty. Many American Indians do not regard this nation as the greatest, except in the sphere of broken promises, treaties, and stolen lands. Those of us who live and have died under its continuing patriotic nationalism of poverty, racism, and dispossession, hardly regard it as a moral compass or beacon of hope. Any nation that regards itself as superior to and separate from others because they were born in another nation, grew up in a different culture, learned a different language, and possess a different consciousness, wilfully destroys what the great Lakota elder Black Elk called the sacred "hoop of life" that connects all tribes of the world.

Michael Yellow Bird,
Canadian Review of American Studies, *2009.*

Listen, if you would, to the wisdom of [US journalist] Milton Mayer, writing back in 1962 a rebuke to JFK [President John F. Kennedy] for his much-celebrated line: "Ask not what your country can do for you, but what you can do for your country."

Mayer would have none of it. "When Mr. Kennedy spoke those words at his inaugural, I knew that I was at odds with a society which did not immediately rebel against them," he wrote. "They are the words of totalitarianism pure; no [President Thomas] Jefferson could have spoken them, and no [Soviet Union premier Nikita] Khrushchev could have spoken them better. Could a man say what Mr. Kennedy said and also say that the difference between us and them is that they believe that man exists for the State and we believe that the State exists for man? He couldn't, but he did. And in doing so, he read me out of society."

When Americans retort that this is still the greatest country in the world, I have to ask why.

Are we the greatest country because we have 10,000 nuclear weapons?

No, that just makes us enormously powerful, with the capacity to destroy the Earth itself.

Are we the greatest country because we have soldiers stationed in more than 120 countries?

No, that just makes us an empire, like the empires of old, only more so.

Are we the greatest country because we are one-twentieth of the world's population but we consume one-quarter of its resources?

No, that just must makes us a greedy and wasteful nation.

Are we the greatest country because the top 1 percent of Americans hoards 34 percent of the nation's wealth, more than everyone in the bottom 90 percent combined?

No, that just makes us a vastly unequal nation.

Are we the greatest country because corporations are treated as real, live human beings with rights?

No, that just enshrines a plutocracy in this country.

Are we the greatest country because we take the best care of our people's basic needs?

No, actually we don't. We're far down the list on health care and infant mortality and parental leave and sick leave and quality of life.

So what exactly are we talking about here?

To the extent that we're a great (not the greatest, mind you: that's a fool's game) country, we're less of a great country today.

Because those things that truly made us great—the system of checks and balances, the enshrinement of our individual rights and liberties—have all been systematically assaulted by [President George W.] Bush and [Vice President Dick] Cheney.

From the Patriot Act to the Military Commissions Act to the new FISA Act, and all the signing statements in between, we are less great today.

From Abu Ghraib [a US Army detention center in Iraq with a history of prisoner abuse] and Bagram Air Force Base [the largest US military base in Afghanistan] and Guantanamo [a controversial US military prison in Cuba], we are less great today.

From National Security Presidential Directive 51 (giving the Executive responsibility for ensuring constitutional government in an emergency) to National Security Presidential Directive 59 (expanding the collection of our biometric data), we are less great today.

From the Joint Terrorism Task Forces to InfraGard and the Terrorist Liaison Officers, we are less great today.

Admit it. We don't have a lot to brag about today.

It is time, it is long past time, to get over the American superiority complex.

It is time, it is long past time, to put patriotism back on the shelf—out of the reach of children and madmen.

Patriotism Should Be Promoted in US Schools

Ernest Smartt

In the following viewpoint, Ernest Smartt argues that American patriotism should be taught in US schools. He says that schools display trophies and awards of the students to instill pride in the school within the students, but many schools are not explaining why the students should be proud of their country. He asserts that when people are proud of their communities, they are more engaged and less apathetic. Smartt fears that children today don't understand why they should be proud of the United States because they mostly hear about the negative aspects of the country and are being taught less and less about the founding documents, Founding Fathers, and the unique freedoms that American citizens possess. Smartt is an educator from Fort Worth, Texas, whose fondest memory is carrying the Olympic torch.

As you read, consider the following questions:

1. According to the author, what did the US Constitution used to be, and what is it now?

2. In Smart's opinion, what would happen if schools began to teach patriotism?

3. What does Smartt think will happen to the United States if patriotism is not once again taught in school?

When you walk into many public schools in America, you will see banners and flags related to the school's pride. That is a wonderful thing to see, and it seems to make one feel a sense of pride just being there. When the trophy case is filled and clean, you sense school spirit and determination. If the trophies are mostly dated within the last 2–5 years, it is clear that something great is happening in that school. Chances are that school has a history of high academic scores as well.

When you walk into the offices of that school you will likely see plaques and photos and other signs and symbols of school pride. These are indications of a school that is making progress on behalf of their students in academics and extra-curricular activities. Often the trophies are not just for sports, but include academic competition winners.

Where there is a spirit of pride, there is also a high standard regarding every aspect of the institution. Too often the spirit and enthusiasm stops at this level. The school may be recognized by the city, county or even the state, but it is usually all about the school. What would happen if these schools began to teach about city, state, and national patriotism? What if the schools were teaching the students to love the place where they live? It is clear that patriotic pride is not being taught, or in many cases even addressed in the curriculum of the schools in America.

Walk into the classrooms of most schools, and you will often discover there is no American flag displayed anywhere in them. Often there may be a paper flag stuck to the wall. If there is a flag, it will usually be one of those little ones that you get free at a fourth of July celebration, and the stick is taped to the wall to hold it up. Quite often you drive by schools and not even see an American or state flag displayed for public viewing on the flag pole. Should patriotism be included in the curriculum of American public schools? Would it make any difference in the academic, ethical and moral standards of those institutions?

Americans Used to be Proud of the Country

There was a time when seeing the American flag was cause for pride. There was a time when heroes were usually connected to some patriotic effort. There was a time when standing to say the Pledge to the flag was a matter of pride, now the most significant discussions surrounding the Pledge are about the right to not say the Pledge at all, and even not standing while it is being said.

We should teach national patriotism in American schools.

It will transform the nation. It is time for America, and the educational system, to return to teaching about what made this Nation so great. It is time to start instilling pride back into the citizens, starting with our youth. It is time to give them some reason for loving this nation.

The Constitution is now a battle ground for defining rights. It used to be the very foundation for freedom. The flag used to have a place because Americans were proud of who they were. Now it is given no respect unless we spoiled Americans get our rights to do whatever we want to do. There is no pride attached to the American flag, unless you have been educated in what makes it a significant symbol of the freedom we have in this great nation.

It Is the Schools' Duty to Teach Patriotism to Students

If we started including patriotism in the curriculum again something big would start happening. If we started letting our students know just how awesome this country really is, the school spirit that you see when you walk into the building, and in the academic standards that such pride creates and excites, would begin to move into the community and city and state. It would begin to create a pride and love for the nation again that spark new energy into the hearts of our youth, resulting in young men and women reclaiming the American dream. Our young people would discover a new motivation for standing up for what is right and good for this nation.

If you really don't know what made this nation great, your generation is one that has been ripped off by the modern age of apathy and greed. If you cannot even see this nation as a great nation, your generation has been robbed of its true heritage. Do a little research and discover why you have the freedom you have. Then realize that what you have discovered is no longer in the books used in the public schools of America.

We should encourage curriculum writers to place the teaching of patriotism back into the teaching. Our youth should be memorizing parts of the founding documents. They need to know what made our early leaders great, and willing to place their lives on the line for freedom. Our children need to know that the signers of the Declaration of Independence were signing possible death warrants on their own lives, all for the freedom we have had for over 200 years. Don't let your children be raised in an era of apathy and greed. Teach them about good pride, patriotism, and the real American way. Let a high standard of ethical and patriotic pride replace greed and selfishness. If patriotism fails to return to the curriculum, America will lose her greatness completely, and fade into immorality and hate and crime.

> *"In public schools across the nation, millions of young children are lined up authoritarian style, told to face an American flag . . . and are then expected to profess their allegiance to it."*

Patriotism Should Not Be Promoted in US Schools

Erik Nielson

In the following viewpoint, Erik Nielson argues that the recitation of the Pledge of Allegiance should not be required by students in US schools. Nielson describes the pledge as a marketing ploy executed by a Christian Socialist in the late nineteenth century to sell flags and capitalize on concerns about increased immigration. In the ensuing years, the author notes that the pledge only grew in its exclusionary aims when clauses defining the flag as American and the nation as existing "under God" were added to emphasize nationalism and bring religion into the public sphere. In light of these origins, he believes that the compulsory nature of the pledge in US schools creates an insincere, mandated patriotism that should be countered by one that is rooted in critical thinking and sincere assessment of one's country. Erik

Nielson is an assistant professor of liberal arts at the University of Richmond and editor of the book Remixing Change: Hip Hop and Obama, A Critical Reader.

As you read, consider the following questions:

1. How long was the original Pledge of Allegiance and what did it say, according to the author?

2. As stated by Nielson, in what years were additional changes made to the pledge?

3. What event identified by the author made it legal for objectors to opt out of the Pledge of Allegiance in school?

Last year [2012], an atheist couple in Massachusetts brought a suit against the Acton-Boxborough Regional School District, arguing that the phrase "under God" in the pledge of allegiance discriminates against their children because, according to their attorney, it "defines patriotism according to a particular religious belief." After they lost their case in Superior Court, they appealed to the Massachusetts Supreme Judicial Court, which agreed to consider their suit. The hearing is scheduled for early next month [May 2013].

Regardless of the outcome—so far, such challenges have ultimately been unsuccessful—the larger issue the case raises is the appropriateness of a pledge of allegiance of any kind in a liberal democracy. It never ceases to amaze me that, day after day, otherwise rational parents allow their impressionable young children to partake in a ritual so rooted in conformity that it seems inimical to the principles of freedom and individualism that underpin our country. And yet, in public schools across the nation, millions of young children are lined up authoritarian style, told to face an American flag dangling somewhere in the room, and are then expected to profess their allegiance to it—and of course to God as well—using words that many are too young understand in the first place. I suspect that most parents assume the pledge has a long and dignified past, that it's part of the American fabric, and are therefore willing to leave it unchallenged. However, its history is not nearly as long or distinguished as people might think.

Bigotry Accompanied the Original Pledge of Allegiance

Indeed, the pledge of allegiance was not conceived by patriotic soldiers making a brave final stand on some cold battlefield during the Revolutionary War, nor was it the inspired creed of our noble Founding Fathers. It was actually written in 1892 by a Christian Socialist, Francis Bellamy, as part of an advertising campaign for *The Youth's Companion*, one of the country's best known and highly regarded magazines. Taking advantage of deep anxiety among Anglo-Saxon Protestants about an increase in immigration during the final decades of the 19th Century, *The Youth's Companion* hatched a scheme to turn nationalism into profit. Through its premium department (essentially a mail order service that sold goods at discounted prices to lure new subscribers), the magazine began selling American flags and promoting the idea of putting one in every school. Seeing the opportunity to link the magazine and its flag drive to a high profile celebration of Columbus Day in October of 1892, one of the magazine's marketers, James Upham, asked Bellamy to craft a pledge of allegiance that would accompany the ceremonial raising of the flag.

Bellamy's original, 23-word pledge read as follows: "I pledge allegiance to my Flag and to the Republic for which it stands, one nation indivisible, with liberty and justice for all." Interestingly, God is nowhere to be found, and neither is any mention of *equality*—perhaps surprising given Bellamy's socialist views. However, like many people who looked scornfully upon America's newest immigrants, Bellamy's Utopian idealism was tempered by his profound xenophobia and big-

A "Cult of the Flag" Surrounds the American Flag

Evidence for the United States' "cult of the flag" abounds. A recent [2007] Pew Research Center poll found that 62 percent of Americans display the flag at home, in their office, or on their vehicles. Another Pew poll reported that 73 percent of Americans thought flag burning should be illegal, and an essay in *Time* magazine noted the use of the word "desecration" in debates over the passage of a constitutional amendment to prohibit flag burning. Frank Trippett, author of the latter, asked, "Philosophically speaking, is it even possible to desecrate the U.S. flag?" His point was that the word "desecration" pertains to holy, sacred, or religious items, thus raising the issue of whether the flag is a religious symbol or a secular one. Although the symbol is ostensibly secular, Trippett's question underscores the religious significance of the national flag for many Americans. As [author of *Who Are We?: The Challenges to America's National Identity* Samuel] Huntington pointed out, "The flag . . . became essentially a religious symbol, the equivalent of the cross for Christians." Given the widespread flying of the U.S. flag both in and outside American churches, it is also arguably the case that the flag's religious overtones have become increasingly intertwined with its secular symbolism.

Gerald R. Webster, Geographical Review, *January 2011.*

otry. Not long after he penned the pledge of allegiance, he made these frightening statements in an editorial for the *Illustrated American*:

A democracy like ours cannot afford to throw itself open to the world. . . . Where all classes of society merge insensibly into one another every alien immigrant of inferior race may bring corruption to the stock. There are races more or less akin to our own whom we may admit freely and get nothing but advantage by the infusion of their wholesome blood. But there are other races, which we cannot assimilate without lowering our racial standard, which we should be as sacred to us as the sanctity of our homes.

Hence, while the pledge of allegiance is widely regarded as a celebration of our patriotism and the "liberty and justice" upon which our nation was founded, its genesis also can be traced to far more sinister fears about the racial, ethnic, and religious contamination that many Americans believed immigrants would bring with them.

Alterations to the Pledge Made It More Acceptable to the Public

Over time, these fears would lead to key changes in the wording of the pledge. First, in the early 1920s, the words "my flag" were changed to "the flag of the United States of America" amidst suspicions that immigrants might subversively interpret "my flag" as a reference to the flag of their homeland. The new wording took care of that. Then, in the late 1940s and early 1950s, as Americans grew increasingly concerned about the threat of communism, there was a movement to add the phrase "under God" to the pledge. This movement, which coincided with a variety of attempts to inject religion into the public sphere in order to differentiate America from the godless communists, was ultimately successful. In 1954, Congress officially recognized the phrase "under God" in the pledge of allegiance—over 60 years after it was originally written and almost two hundred years after our founding fathers labored to establish a nation that kept the church and state separate.

Today, regardless of their religious beliefs, public school students in most states are required by law to endure the pledge of allegiance, complete with its State-sponsored affirmation of God. While there are generally exceptions carved out for objectors (thanks to a 1943 Supreme Court ruling that said children couldn't be forced to recite it), they must nevertheless watch as their classmates stand in unison and, with hands over hearts, utter a government-mandated pledge of loyalty to the United States. Since such a ritual tends to evoke images of a fascist regime rather than a modern democracy, perhaps it's also worth noting that the prescribed salute to the flag was originally an extended arm, hand out, and palm upward, not unlike the Nazi salute.

This similarity in stance to the German counterpart—and of course, the compulsory nature of the exercise—raised concerns over the appearance of the pledge, so in 1942 the salute was modified to the hand-over-heart pose we recognize today.

Patriotism Should Not Be Mandated by Schools

But a new salute doesn't hide the old fears and prejudices that helped shape the pledge of allegiance, nor does it make a compulsory affirmation of liberty any less ironic. Perhaps unsurprisingly, as immigration moves to the forefront of the national debate and we face the possibility that millions of undocumented immigrants could soon become American citizens, calls for making the pledge of allegiance mandatory have recently surfaced in Michigan and Nebraska, two of the few remaining states without laws requiring the pledge.

While there is hope in the upcoming Massachusetts case, parents don't have to wait for the courts or lawmakers. Instead, they can take a pledge of their own: that they will no longer condone this daily exercise in nationalistic indoctrination and religious inculcation. That's what my wife and I have done—we strongly encourage our two young children to abstain from any part of the pledge of allegiance. It's not easy. They are the only ones in their classes who don't participate, and I know it has made them uncomfortable. But as they begin to understand that thinking for themselves is the true embodiment of liberty, I am hopeful that they will arrive at a patriotism that is honest and critical, not one that has been foisted upon them.

> *"Our soldiers are unequivocally quali-*
> *fied recipients of all the love, goodwill,*
> *compassion, and loyalty that we have*
> *always identified as our most virtuous*
> *and generous qualities."*

Supporting the Troops Unites the American Public

Ronnie Polaneczky

In the following viewpoint, Ronnie Polaneczky describes the near national consensus of support for the US troops and asserts that the majority of the people who express concern for the troops do so in part to feel a sense of unification with their fellow Americans. This desire for unification stems in large part from the current divisive political climate, according to the author's observations. This division, Polaneczky argues, obscures one overarching similarity among all Americans: their generosity. This generosity, in the author's eyes, is the other factor leading to widespread support for American troops; Americans want to give to those who deserve it, and they see the troops as a worthy receiver of this charity. Polaneczky is a columnist for the Philadelphia Daily News *who has won awards for her writing and contributed works to a wide range of publications.*

Ronnie Polaneczky, "Why We So Strongly Support Our Troops," Philly.com, May 30, 2012. Copyright © 2012 by Ronnie Polaneczky. Used by permission. All rights reserved.

As you read, consider the following questions:

1. How do American views of the troops today compare with views of troops in the past, according to the author?

2. As stated by the author, how do troop-supporting Americans feel about the division of the country today?

3. What is the "feel-good trifecta" into which the author states the troops fall?

You don't have to be a student of military conflict to know that America's high opinion of our troops, which soared during the World Wars and the Korean conflict, plunged during the Vietnam era.

Returning soldiers were held accountable for the president's decisions. Some have never recovered from feeling the contempt of their countrymen for being in the wrong war, under the wrong leader.

Things couldn't be more different today. Regardless of where individuals stand in their opinion of the conflicts in the Middle East, there's a national sense that the men and women fighting there are not to be blamed for it, but honored for having signed up.

To get a sense of how everyday Americans stand behind our men and women in uniform, scroll through a website like troopssupport.com. It's a directory of organizations that provide everything from free lawn care and baby showers for veterans and their families to job training and new homes for soldiers wounded in action.

This is wonderful, obviously. But it raises the question: Why have we embraced our soldiers so tightly this time around? Other than an appreciation for their sacrifice, is something else going on?

Support for the Troops Accompanies Opposition to War

In the early days of the [Iraq] antiwar movement, expressions of support for the troops seemed to preface nearly any and all statements of opposition to war that were made before the mainstream press—and for good reason. As a journalist for the *San Francisco Chronicle* reported, Eddie Veder, the lead singer of the rock band Pearl Jam, was jeered and booed at a 2003 concert in Denver, Colorado when he criticised the war and the president [George W. Bush] on stage. It was not until he thought to add, "Just to clarify . . . we support the troops," that cheers and applause erupted from the audience again—enabling the show to go on. This charged and emotional exchange, while seemingly spontaneous, followed what . . . was becoming an all too familiar script for anyone voicing dissent—in which supporting the troops became, more or less, a condition of legitimate dissent.

Tina Managhan, Geopolitics, *2011.*

Americans Long for a Connection with Their Fellow Citizens

The questions began to consume me a few years back, after I wrote a column about The Liberty Limited, a temporary, multicar train that was assembled by Bennett Levin, a former Philly L&I commissioner and self-made millionaire.

The Liberty Limited carried wounded soldiers from Washington and from Bethesda, Md., to Philly for the Army-Navy game. I volunteered and saw firsthand the joy of troops reveling in their break from hospitals and rehab.

The column elicited huge response—more than a thousand emails, plus letters and phone calls—from readers eager to declare their love for our soldiers. Many were actively showing it, too, with single efforts like Levin's.

The do-gooders ranged from big-hearted teens, to single moms, to Harvard-trained shrinks and celebrities. Many spent substantial time, money and prayers on men and women they'd never met.

So I asked more than a hundred of these folks, "What is it about the troops that moves you so deeply?"

The thread connecting their responses revealed itself over time, in bits and pieces, beneath the surface of every phone conversation and email exchange:

"Because holding the troops in high regard is about the only thing that unites Americans today. And I am dying to feel united with my fellow Americans about something we agree upon unequivocally."

Generosity Is an American Trait

These are tough times in our republic, painfully fractured by politics, economics and culture.

We can't agree upon what it means to be an American. Or a patriot. Or a defender of family values. Or a protector of civil and constitutional rights. For so many of the troop-supporters I interviewed, the notion that America is as divided as countries they believed to be less special than the United States was both scary and disorienting.

Where they regained their balance was in the belief that we are united in conviction that the troops deserve our support. And, oh, how good it felt to agree, as a nation, about something so big and important.

"See," they thought, without even knowing they were thinking it, "THIS is what it is to be American: It is to be one who is willing to serve—and one who is willing to serve those who serve."

They viewed this generosity as an American trait but had become cynical and wary about giving not just their money but their very caring to causes that may not be worthy of the love. And it was, indeed, love that they were eager to give.

But not if it made fools of them.

That's a sentiment shared by most Americans. It's why we tend to embrace, say, charities that help children, who didn't ask to be born into whatever dire circumstances they find themselves. And it's why we aren't so fired up over causes that help, say, unwed mothers, prison inmates or others whom we feel very much had a say in creating their sad fortunes.

Our troops fall into a unique category: They are often in tough situations they did not create; they persevere heroically; and they do it for the sake of country.

It's a feel-good trifecta.

As a result, our soldiers are unequivocally qualified recipients of all the love, goodwill, compassion and loyalty that we have always identified as our most virtuous and generous qualities.

I think that our need to give wholeheartedly to others has for years been so stopped up, argued over or misdirected that it was bound to explode the way it has with support of the troops.

Their ever-presence in our headlines and their constant, worthy need, leads Americans back to what we believe is our best, collective self.

> "The troops are engaged in actions that
> are harmful to the American people,
> including most of the people who have
> a reverential attitude toward them."

Supporting the Troops Puts the American Public at Risk

Jacob G. Hornberger

In the following viewpoint, Jacob G. Hornberger notes that in general, the American people hold US military troops in high regard and offer unconditional support to them and their causes. However, he contends, the people have erred in this support because, instead of protecting the American people, the troops create a situation where Americans are more likely to be attacked. The author compares the actions of the troops to poking a hornets' nest, saying that the military's presence and actions in other countries inflame anti-American sentiment, particularly following the 9/11 terrorist attacks. Regardless of the fact that the troops may just be following orders, as many supporters contend, Hornberger remains steadfast in his belief that the troops enforce these policies of their own free will and must be held accountable. Hornberger is president of the Future of Freedom Foundation, a libertarian organization.

As you read, consider the following questions:

1. What is the response of the family when asked about the weekly hornet stings in the author's hypothetical situation comparing the troops to hornets?

2. As stated by the author, why does getting into US foreign policy make supporters of the troops uncomfortable?

3. What are some of the programs identified by the author as enforced by the troops and the source of anger toward the United States?

One of the most fascinating phenomena of our time is the extreme reverence that the American people have been taught to have for the military. Wherever you go—airports, sports events, church—there is a god-like worship of the military.

"Let us all stand and express our sincerest thanks to our troops for the wonderful service they perform for our country," declare the sports broadcasters.

"Let us pray for the troops, especially those in harm's way," church ministers exhort their parishioners.

"Let us give a big hand to our troops who are traveling with us today," exclaim airline officials.

Every time I see this reverence for the military being expressed, I wonder if people ever give any thought to what exactly the troops are doing. No one seems to ask that question. It just doesn't seem to matter. The assumption is that whatever the troops are doing, they are protecting our "rights and freedoms." As one sports broadcaster I recently heard put it, "We wouldn't be here playing this game if it weren't for the troops."

The Troops Should Be Supported Before They Become Soldiers

Standing with the troops in a progressive fashion would be to support young men and women before they become soldiers. The material benefits now made available to entice young men and women into the all-volunteer military should be made available to all citizens as a matter of course. These benefits, which provide pathways to a more sustainable livelihood and claim stake in US society, might still be linked to a commitment to national service, although that service might also include participation in AmeriCorps, the Peace Corps, or a reconstituted Civilian Conservation Corps. The idea here is not to demean military service as a calling or career. Although a non-militaristic society and a healthy democracy require both a smaller standing army and a less powerful military industrial sector, the animating impulse to reform should not be to debilitate the military, but rather to decouple the incentive structures that make military service the only readily plausible avenue for citizenry belonging. Soldiering in a democracy, defending the country against external threat, should be seen as a noble service—just not uniquely more honorable than other contributions to our common revolutionary project, deepening and extending the democratic experiment launched at the United States' founding.

Gerard Huiskamp, New Political Science, *September 2011.*

There is at least one big problem with this phenomenon, however: The troops are engaged in actions that are harmful to the American people, including most of the people who have a reverential attitude toward them.

The Troops Stir Up Trouble

Consider the following hypothetical. Suppose a family lives out in the country on a 50-acre spread in the middle of a wooded area. In the trees are dozens of hornets' nests. The hornets leave the family alone because the family leaves the hornets' nests alone.

One day U.S. troops arrive, come on to the property, and begin poking every hornets' nest they can find. For the next several days, the members of the family and their friends and visitors are stung by the hornets.

The following week, the troops arrive and do the same thing, with the same results. This goes on indefinitely.

Suppose we were to encounter the family and ask them how they feel about the troops. We could easily imagine them saying, "Oh, we love the troops and we support them. Without them, we wouldn't have this nice property. Thank goodness for the troops because they are keeping us free."

What about all weekly stings from the hornets? We could easily imagine the family responding, "Oh, that's not the troops' fault. For some reason, the hornets are just mad these days, but it has nothing to do with the fact that the troops are poking their nests. Anyway, the troops are just following orders. It's not their fault. We love the troops."

Does that make any sense? It seems to me that when people are doing the right thing, they are entitled to be supported. But when they're engaged in wrongful or harmful conduct, then they shouldn't be supported. Why should the military be exempt from normal moral and ethical principles?

Americans Support Those Who Cause the Problems

Consider the threat of terrorism, which Americans have lived under now for some 11 years. Did you ever think that 9/11 [terror attacks] would change our country so fundamentally?

There wasn't any "war on terrorism" before 9/11. Torture and assassination weren't official policy. There was no detention center at Guantanamo Bay. There were no official kidnappings, rendition, and torture partnerships with brutal dictatorial regimes. There was no indefinite incarceration without trial.

So, why must everything be different just because of 9/11? Why can't we live in a normally functioning society, one in which people are not living under the constant fear of terrorism and one in which the government isn't adopting and employing permanent "emergency" powers that constitute severe infringements on the freedoms of the people.

What was it that produced the anger and rage that brought on 9/11? Was it hatred for America's "freedom and values," as U.S. officials maintain? Or was it anger and rage arising from what the troops and other U.S. officials were doing to people in the months and years leading up to 9/11?

That obviously gets us into U.S. foreign policy, an area that makes many people who support the troops very uncomfortable. Why? Because if they conclude that the troops are doing things to people overseas that are producing the anti-American anger and rage that culminates in anti-American terrorism, then that presents a problem for them. How do they in good conscience continue supporting the people who are causing their problems?

The Troops Enforce Foreign Policy

Yet, the reality is that the troops are doing things to people overseas that are making people angry at the United States. Examples include the invasions and occupations of Iraq and Afghanistan and ever-increasing drone assassinations. As everyone knows, such actions have succeeded in killing and maiming hundreds of thousands of people, including women and children. On top of that has been the torture, the kidnappings, Gitmo, the support of brutal dictatorships and the Israeli government, the U.S. troops on Islamic holy lands, the il-legal no-fly zone over Iraq, the sanctions that killed hundreds of thousands of Iraqi children, and the current sanctions on Iran. It's the troops who enforce many of those programs.

Now, it might be said that the troops aren't at fault be-cause they're just following orders. Even if that's true, is that any reason to support them? For one thing, no one forced them to join an organization that would require them to do whatever they were ordered to do. They did that on their own volition.

Moreover, even though they're following orders, the fact remains that what they're doing is nonetheless counterproduc-tive to the best interests of the American people. That is, for those of us who want a normally functioning society, rather than the aberrant post-9/11 society in which we now live, what the troops are doing is an obstacle to the achievement of our goal, whether they are doing it willingly or simply on or-ders of their commanders.

Americans Must Confront the Root Causes of Their Problems

For those Americans who like the direction our country has been taking for the past 11 years and would like things to continue as they are, the best thing they can do is simply con-tinue supporting the troops.

But for people who are sick and tired of all this, for them it's necessary to confront the root causes of America's prob-lems. And like it or not, one of the root causes of America's woes is the U.S. military establishment and the entire national-security state, not only with respect to the anti-American an-ger and hatred they produce by their actions overseas but also by contributing to the out-of-control spending and debt that now constitute a grave threat to the economic well-being of our nation.

Why would anyone want to support people who are doing things that are detrimental to us and our country?

Periodical and Internet Sources Bibliography

The following articles have been selected to supplement the diverse views presented in this chapter.

Amir Azarvan	"Support Our Troops . . . Until They Come Home," *New Politics*, Summer 2009.
Warren J. Blumenfeld	"I Don't Pledge Allegiance (to Any Flag)," *Humanist*, November/December 2013.
Joseph Epstein	"Whose Country 'Tis of Thee?," *Commentary*, November 2011.
Todd Gitlin	"Patriotism," *Chronicle of Higher Education*, August 12, 2011.
Gerard Huiskamp	"'Support the Troops!': The Social and Political Currency of Patriotism in the United States," *Political Science*, September 1, 2010.
Wilfred M. McClay	"Memorializing September 11th," *National Affairs*, Fall 2011.
John Nichols	"For Progressive Patriotism," *Nation*, February 2, 2009.
David Pluviose	"Obama the Patriot," *Diverse: Issues in Higher Education*, February 14, 2013.
Andrew Roberts	"Patriotism, Allegiance and the Nation State," *New Criterion*, January 2013.
John Spiri	"Patriotism and Education," *Dissident Voice*, June 2009.

CHAPTER 4

Can American Values Bridge Cultural Divides?

Chapter Preface

A March 2013 survey conducted by the Public Religion Research Institute (PRRI) reported that less than one-third (32 percent) of Americans believe that immigration is "changing their communities a lot"; though 46 percent contend that immigration is "changing American society a lot." The PRRI, which polled 4,500 Americans from various demographic backgrounds, found that Americans generally had a positive view of immigrants. A majority (54 percent) think that "the growing number of newcomers from other countries helps strengthen American society," yet a sizable minority (40 percent) indicated that "newcomers threaten traditional American customs and values." The nonpartisan Pew Research Center gathered similar results from its own 2012 poll on immigration. The Pew results showed the split to be 48 percent (no) to 46 percent (yes) on the more pointed question of whether immigrants threaten American values. According to the Pew findings, lower income and education levels were a correlating factor in respondents who agreed with the statement that immigrants are a threat to US customs and values.

Writer Amit Ghate claims those defending the notion that newcomers threaten the ideals and values of the United States are a "rearguard" holding on to a stagnant view of national identity. In a November 12, 2012, opinion piece for *Forbes*, he draws on historical precedents to illustrate that progressive cultures commonly adapt to new ideas and foreign influences. Hoping the nation will choose to avoid insular decay by rejecting its melting pot image, Ghate asserts, "Let's not succumb to the specious idea of demographic determinism to radically limit immigration. Instead let's demonstrate the moral confidence, and intellectual rigor, to bid welcome to all." This sentiment is shared by many who insist the United States has always been a nation of immigrants and benefited from ethnic diversity.

Not everyone agrees with the optimism of this open-door outlook. In a July 19, 2004, article published on a number of websites, cultural commentator and lecturer Frosty Wooldridge espoused his notion that lax US immigration laws were a disservice to the nation and the security of its people. Claiming that the new influx of immigrants were different than previous waves, Wooldridge maintains that modern immigrants have no desire to embrace the American Dream to build a stronger nation; instead they seek only to profit from economic opportunity. He contends that the media elites are blind to this fact because they are enamored with catchwords such as "multiculturalism" even while the population at large has no interest in broadening the country's already diverse traditions. He does not want to see the United States become a land of coexisting cultures but a nation of one shared culture. "American culture is worth preserving," Wooldridge trumpets, and in his view, "Immigration laws should ensure that those who seek to live permanently on American territory be willing to adopt and preserve its culture."

In the following chapter, authors take up the issue of immigration and American values. Some view national culture as a unified trait worth preserving, while others put forth the argument that culture is always evolving, and attempts to crystalize it will drain it of its value. These opinions reveal a country divided over heritage and the manner in which traditional values should be interpreted to carry the United States through the twenty-first century.

> "As soon as Muhammad died, his reli-
> gion of peace became a house of inter-
> nal war."

Islam Is Incompatible with American Values

Amil Imani

*In the following viewpoint, Amil Imani, an Iranian-born Ameri-
can citizen, urges Americans to be cautious of Islam and its followers. He argues that despite Islamists' claims, Islam is not a
religion of peace, but rather a political ideology of oppression
and hatred. He points to specific text in the Quran as examples
of this intolerance and hatred. He says that the politically correct
attitude toward Islam in the United States is very dangerous because it has allowed the barbaric religion, which practices Sharia
law—rules that oppress women and children—to grow in the
United States, a country that was founded on freedom and fairness to all people. Imani is a prodemocracy activist, columnist,
novelist, and translator who speaks out for the people of his native land of Iran.*

As you read, consider the following questions:

1. According to Amil Imani, how did the Islamic prophet
   Muhammad deal with nonbelievers?

2. The Egyptian government claims that the Muslim Brotherhood is outlawed in Egypt, but according to Imani what percentage of the Egyptian parliament is made up of the Muslim Brotherhood?

3. According to the author, why is Sharia law unfair, who is it unfair to, and how are these laws different from laws in the United States?

Islam has spawned many sects that are master practitioners of the art of double standards. As far as Muslims are concerned, what is good for Muslims is not good for the non-Muslims; and what is bad for Muslims is good for non-Muslims.

What complicates matters is that there is no way of knowing which of the dozens of at-each-other's-throat sects is the legitimate Islam. As soon as Muhammad [founder of Islam] died, his religion of peace became a house of internal war: jockeying for power and leadership started, sects formed and splintered into sub-sects, and bloodletting began in earnest.

The internal infighting in Islam is presently playing in full color—in red—most dramatically, in the Iraqi theater. Shiite [faction of Islam] raid Sunni [faction of Islam] civilians, slaughter them like sheep, and toss their bodies like trash in the streets or the rivers. The Sunnis return the favor with just as much viciousness and savagery.

Question: If this is the way these Muslims treat each other, how would they deal with the infidels [non-Islamists] if they had the chance?

Answer: These devoted followers of Muhammad would deal with the infidels exactly the way Muhammad did: behead the non-believers, take them as slaves to hold or sell, or make them pay back-breaking jizya—poll taxes.

Examining the Arguments
of Islamic Apologists

Some may object that writings like this are little more than hate-mongering and fanning the fire that rages between Islam and the non-Islamic world. They may further play the Islamic apologists' few, well-worn propaganda cards as evidence for their contention that Islam is not what its detractors claim.

Here are the few favorite cards.

* "There is no compulsion in religion," says the Quran [Islam's holy book] (But the full context is never shown.)

* Islam means "peace," so Islam is a religion of peace.

* "For you, your religion, and for me, my religion," Muhammad reportedly said.

The Muslims and their apologists quickly run out of their few cards, and the rest of the Islamic deck is all about intolerance, hatred and violence toward the infidels, toward all others who are not true Muslims, and even toward those who consider themselves Muslims. Shiites, for instance, judge the Sunnis as traitors to Islam, and Sunnis condemn the Shiites as heretics. Each side deems the other worthy of death and hellfire.

This internecine Islamic war of the religion of peace is not confined to the Shiite-Sunni divide. There are so many internal divisions within each side that listing and describing them comprehensively would be an encyclopedic work.

So, who is right? What are the facts about Islam and how does Islam impact the ever-shrinking village Earth and its inhabitants? Admittedly, this is a huge question and cannot be answered satisfactorily in one [viewpoint]. However, some facts can be presented to help the reader decide.

There is no need to belabor the point that Islam is not, and has never been, a religion of peace. The word Islam is derived from taslim, which purely means "submission," while the term for "peace" is solh. Another derivation of the word taslim is "salema", which means "good health" and so on.

Islamist Lawfare Threatens Free Speech

The war against Islamism is as much a war of ideas as it is a physical battle, and therefore the dissemination of information in the free world is paramount. The manipulation of Western court systems, the use of Western "hate speech laws" and other products of political correctness to destroy the very principles that democracies stand for, must be countered.

Unfortunately, Islamist lawfare [using the legal system to wage war] is beginning to limit and control public discussion of Islam, particularly as it pertains to comprehending the threat posed by Islamic terrorist entities. As such, the Islamist lawfare challenge presents a direct and real threat not only to our constitutional rights, but also to our national security.

Yet, what are the positions of the American Civil Liberties Union and the Center for Constitutional Rights (CCR) on this issue? Where is the international media? Why is this issue being met with virtual silence. . . ?

Some have argued that the anti-Americanism of radical Islamists has little to do with anti-imperialism, but reflects a profound contempt for the liberal social democratic society we have built and its emphasis on individual liberties and freedoms. Freedom of expression is the cornerstone of democratic liberty—it is a freedom that Western civilizations have over time paid for with blood. We must not give it up so easily.

Brooke Goldstein and Aaron Eitan Meyer,
ILSA Journal of International and Comparative Law,
Spring 2009.

Islam Is Based on Violence and Oppression

Irrespective of what the term Islam may mean, the facts on the ground conclusively demonstrate Islam's violent nature from its very inception. No need to go back to the time of Muhammad and examine the historical records. Just a few contemporary events should make the point.

Here is a partial list: the savage Shiite-Sunni bloodletting in Iraq; the barbarism of the resurgent Taliban in Afghanistan; the genocide in Sudan's Darfur region; the Somali killings; the Iranian mullahs' murder of their own people and support of mischief abroad; the incessant terrorist acts of Hamas, Hezbollah and Islamic Jihad on Israel, and numerous fatwas [Islamic rulings] on infidels and the apostates; the bombing of Shiite mosques in Pakistan and Iraq and the Shiite retaliation against soft, innocent and civilian targets.

Clearly, there is no place on the planet where Muslims reside that is in peace from the religion of peace. America, Spain, France, Netherlands, England, Thailand, India and Indonesia have already been attacked, while others, such as Denmark, have been threatened and sanctioned.

Stretching the benefit of the doubt beyond limits, one may believe that all these acts of horrors are committed by a small minority of thugs and radicals who happened to be Muslims. Fine, let us ignore all those "fringes" for now—those who are giving Islam a bad reputation. And never mind Saudi Arabia, the cradle of barbarism, fixed in formaldehyde since Islam's inception. Also, let us overlook the dastardly Shiite fanatics presently ruling (ruining) the great nation of Iran. Iranian Shiite Hitlerists are hell-bent on wiping Israel off the face of the planet, while viciously devastating Iran's own largest minority—the Baha'is, people universally recognized as law-abiding and peaceful.

Would someone account for what is happening in the "civilized" Islamic country of Egypt? The world owes Egypt a debt of gratitude for giving it the Muslim Brotherhood [Islamic political group]—the lead promoter of Sunni hatred toward the infidels, with chapters and front organizations in much of the world. With typical hypocrisy, the Egyptian government claims that the Muslim Brotherhood is outlawed, when, in actuality, the Brotherhood holds twenty-five percent of the seats in the Egyptian parliament. The same country that gave the world vicious American-killers like Al-Zawahiri is the recipient of huge largess from the American taxpayer. Islamic rules are called Sharia law or the Islamic law. Sharia law is a misnomer, for laws must be squarely based on justice and fairness to all, while Sharia law is nothing more than a primitive set of dogma stipulated by men for the benefit of Muslim men.

Sharia law [law of Islam] disenfranchises women from their legitimate equal rights with men; prescribes barbaric punishments such as stoning, amputation of limbs and death. Sharia law, contrary to what its advocates claim, does not limit application of its draconian provisions to Muslims only: it considers any and all disputes involving Muslims with non-Muslims also in its purview to adjudicate. Sharia law is inherently arbitrary, obsolete, and discriminatory to the extreme. Wherever Sharia law rules, injustice prevails. Non-Muslims, women, and even children are victimized by its biased and cruel provisions.

Sharia law represents a twist to the concept of Blind Justice: It is indeed blind to justice. Even a cursory examination of Sharia's family law, for instance, proves unequivocally its blindness to justice: it makes the shameful past laws, such as Jim Crow laws, seem as paragons of fairness by comparison.

These are the conditions on the ground wherever Sharia rules. Violence of all forms is endemic to Islamic law and is not confined to any fringes. Sharia law itself is the fringe—a fringe that is oppressive, hateful of others and violent to the core.

Presently, fanatical Islam is lashing out with mad fury before its own final demise. The "infidel" world has been complicit in the surge of Islamism through its mistakes, complacency, and greed. Warning: Islam is not a religion but a political ideology which incites hate, violence, intolerance and terror. Islamists are terminators. You cannot bargain with them. You cannot reason with them. They do not feel pity or remorse, or fear. And they absolutely will not stop, ever, until all the infidels are dead or have submitted to Islam. The only language the Islamists understand is the language of force.

In non-Muslim lands, Islamism, flush with *Petrodollars* has been accelerating in its drive for the world Caliphate and is moving at the speed of light by building more mosques, printing more indoctrinating Islamic books, imposing more its presence in the western culture, in our schools and university campuses, bullying, intimidating and challenging more Christians and other peaceful people of faith and by using our democratic laws against us.

In the Islamdom, they can dish out insults to non-Muslims; arrest Christians, Bahia's or the Jews just for praying. They can confiscate their Holy books and toss them in the trash. They call the Jews pigs and monkeys, and spit on anyone that isn't Muslim. But they go into frenzies of righteous outrage at the slightest criticism of their barbaric and highly dangerous beliefs.

The United States Must Stop Protecting Dangerous Islamists

They never need to challenge the existing political order in our country, but can achieve all their goals without bothering or violating the Constitution of the U.S. because that Constitution guarantees complete government non-interference toward religion. Finally and the most important element perhaps is the extreme coziness and appeasement by the current U.S. administration towards Islam, Muslims and radical Muslims which will recklessly and unknowingly drag the whole country and her citizens into an everlasting Islamic inferno, an inferno similar to the Islamic Republic of Iran and other Islamic terrorist countries.

A constitutional amendment must be passed quickly defining Islam as a hostile political force with a global totalitarian agenda, and as such is totally inimical to our constitution and our national security, and that further to this definition, all practicing Muslims must either renounce this cult or be deported to their countries of origin, and all mosques must be demolished, since their goal is to propagate political propaganda, which has nothing whatsoever to do with 'religion'—let alone one of 'peace'. That's going to be the final 'solution' for Islam in America.

"Fight and kill the disbelievers wherever you find them, take them captive, harass them, lie in wait and ambush them using every stratagem of war." Qur'an:9:5

"Fight those who do not believe until they all surrender, paying the protective tax in submission." Qur'an:9:29

We must also end the deadly practice of "Political Correctness." Truth, only naked truth, can set us free. And freedom is our greatest gift of life. Life without freedom is death disguised as life. Remember [US attorney and politician] Patrick Henry's cry: Give me liberty or give me death. Humanity cannot afford, and must not ignore, the emergence of the latest threat to its very existence on this planet. We must fight for life, for liberty, for freedom and end the nightmare of Islamic hellfire.

| "These false and offensive [anti-Islamic] ideas communicate to the world's Muslims that America is against them."

Anti-Islamic Sentiment Is Incompatible with American Values

Matthew Duss

On September 11, 2012, the US embassy in Benghazi, Libya, was attacked, four Americans were killed, and Libyan guards were injured. In the following viewpoint, Matthew Duss argues that anti-Islamic sentiment in the United States, as seen in the video blamed for inciting these attacks, violates the right of freedom of religion. While Duss places the blame for the attacks and the following riots squarely on the participating individuals, he still asserts that those who perpetuate Islamophobia in the United States add to the damaging narrative that the United States and Islam are inherently opposed. Duss urges the strong condemnation of anti-Islam individuals in accordance with the American value of freedom of religion. Duss works as a policy analyst with the Center for American Progress' national security team.

As you read, consider the following questions:

1. According to the author, what do "democratic values allow for," and what do they never include?

2. What was the stated intent of the producers of the movie *The Innocence of Muslims*, according to Duss?

3. What beliefs does Duss state that all anti-Islamists share?

The ongoing demonstrations against U.S. embassies in the Middle East, which tragically resulted in the deaths of four American diplomats alongside a number of Libyan defenders last week [September 11, 2012], represent a considerable challenge to U.S. diplomacy. The protests also demonstrate the power of one insidious aspect of social media designed to spark the most incendiary response—ugly and false propaganda designed to travel at light speed across international boundaries from one country that respects free speech to many others that are only now learning how to deal with the free flow of information.

It's important to locate blame for the riots where it belongs—with the rioters and those who are cynically exploiting an offensive, poorly made YouTube video to aggravate preexisting grievances and incite violence. Democratic values allow for the full expression of grievances, freedom of speech, and political debate. But whatever the merits of the disagreement, the right of free speech never includes violent actions, criminal assaults, and lawlessness. Five diplomats at work in the evening must always expect their host government to protect them from a disorderly mob.

But it's also important to understand the ideology behind the video that sparked the protests, as articulated by those who made it, and the connections that exist between them and the broader Islamophobia network in the United States, as described in the Center for American Progress's 2011 report, "Fear, Inc.: The Roots of the Islamophobia Network in America."

The Islamophobia Network Promotes Hate

Originally the maker of the film was reported as someone named "Sam Bacile." Bacile said in an interview with *The Wall Street Journal* that the film, titled "The Innocence of Muslims," was intended to showcase his view of Islam as a hateful religion. "Islam is a cancer," Bacile said. "The movie is a political movie. It's not a religious movie."

Authorities now believe Bacile is really Nakoula Basseley Nakoula, a Coptic-Egyptian American with a criminal history that includes bank fraud and narcotics.

Yesterday the *Long Beach Press-Telegram* reported that "The Innocence of Muslims" was produced by a southern California-based Christian nonprofit called Media for Christ. Fundamentalist Christian activist Steve Klein, who hosts a video program produced by Media for Christ, acknowledges being a consultant for the movie. "Our intent was to reach out to the small minority of very dangerous people in California and try to shock them into understanding how dangerous Islam is," Klein told a local news station.

In one video on his website The Way, Klein displays his paranoia and complete misunderstanding of the wide and varied world of Islam when he warns that "what we're seeing going on in Egypt translates throughout all of the world." He says, "Muslim Brotherhood [one of the largest and most influential Islamic political organizations in the world], [former Iranian president Mahmoud] Ahmadinejad, doesn't matter if they're Sunni, Shi'ite, Sufi [branches of Islam], eventually they're gonna attack and erupt."

The *Press-Telegram* also reports that both Media for Christ and The Way "are run by Joseph Abdelmasih of Arcadia, who is listed as chief executive officer for both entities, and presi-

The United States Is More Open to Islam than Is Western Europe

Notwithstanding the common signs of ethnocentrism occasioned by the emergence of Islam in the United States and Western Europe, the two locales exhibit strikingly different responses to Islam in the public square. These differences may owe something to the very different profiles of Muslim communities in the two environments, differences in national origin, race, ethnicity, language, socioeconomic status and the like. Yet the most important factor that determines whether Muslims are free to build mosques appears to be neither public opinion nor the composition of the Muslim population, but rather the regime that governs religion and state. Largely a product of national experience, this set of norms and procedures extends beyond an abstract commitment to religious freedom and equality to encompass policies and processes governing specific religious issues. When it comes to mosque construction, the regime in the United States provides strong legal backing to religious newcomers that favors and reinforces their capacity to create institutions. In Western Europe, where regimes still reflect the interests of older and more well-established religious traditions, religious newcomers like Muslims find themselves dependent on widely varying local conditions and sentiments. Hence Muslims in Western Europe are often handicapped in creating a religious infrastructure. Given the way regimes are rooted in national development patterns, these differences are unlikely to diminish much over the short run.

Kenneth D. Wald,
Politics, Religion, and Ideology, *September 2011.*

dent of Media for Christ, public records show." Joseph Abdel-masih is also known as Joseph Nasrallah, also a Coptic Egyptian-American. On the 2010 anniversary of the September 11 attacks, he spoke at a rally near Ground Zero organized by Pamela Geller and Robert Spencer, both major figures in the Islamophobia network.

That rally was designed as a protest against the so-called "Ground Zero Mosque," which is in reality an Islamic cultural center located several blocks away from the former site of the World Trade Center. The center's developer, Sharif El-Gamal, told the Associated Press that the center is modeled after the Jewish Community Center on Manhattan's Upper West Side, where he lives. The center opened its doors last year [2011].

But Nasrallah sees it differently because of his extreme prejudice against Islam. "They are using taqiya" (an Arabic term describing an Islamic concept of dissimulation or deception to avoid religious persecution). "They are using deceiving. They are lying against Pamela Geller, they are lying against Robert Spencer. They are lying lying lying!"

Anti-Islamists Violate Religious Freedom

What all of these activists share is a belief that the Islamic faith and Western culture are irreconcilable, and that conflict between the two is inevitable. As in Manhattan; Temecula, California; and Murfreesboro, Tennessee, mosques are seen as beachheads for an invading army, and American Muslims are seen as potential sleeper agents, willing to use any deception to transform America into an Islamic state.

In addition to threatening to marginalize and alienate a growing sector of Americans, the vast majority of whom are deeply committed to American values and ideals, these false and offensive ideas communicate to the world's Muslims that America is against them, and affirm the rhetoric of radical extremists who claim there can be no peace between Islam and the West.

Sadly, too many mainstream conservatives in our country cavort with members of the Islamophobia network in the United States such as Pamela Geller, Robert Spencer, Frank Gaffney, and others, lending credence to their paranoid rants and encouragement to the likes of Steve Klein and Nakoula Basseley Nakoula who produced and promoted a video designed to spark violent reaction. Such ugly propaganda and its creators should be strongly condemned alongside those who manipulated the situation for their own political ends in the Middle East. So, too, should the supporters of Islamophobia who create a breeding ground for hate by denigrating one of the world's great religions and insult the sacrifice of our military and diplomatic corps by violating America's core value of religious freedom.

| "With so many Americans losing their homes and unable to find jobs, it is outrageous to say Hispanics still take jobs no one else will do."

Illegal Immigrants Do Not Embrace American Values

Walter Rodgers

In the following viewpoint, Walter Rodgers posits that American values are being corroded by illegal Hispanic immigrants that choose not to learn English or assimilate into the culture. Many of these immigrants, he argues, are uneducated and have no intention of educating their children in the United States; he believes this will flood the nation with uneducated Spanish-speaking immigrants that refuse to accept American values. The author says that allowing these illegal immigrants to come to the United States in masses is akin to committing national suicide. Rodgers writes a biweekly column for the Christian Science Monitor *and is a former senior international correspondent for* CNN.

As you read, consider the following questions:

1. According to US Census statistics, what percent of California will be Latino by the year 2042?

2. What does professor Lawrence Harrison of Tufts University say about some of the fourth- and fifth-generation Hispanics in California?

3. What does the author think Congress should do to help reduce illegal immigration in the United States?

Walking the sandy beachfront in this ultra-affluent city [Santa Barbara, California], I chanced upon two Hispanic men rummaging through the trash. Startled at the sight, I stared momentarily. One of them yelled at me, "You look now, but in 50 years we will own all this!" Given the tsunami of illegal immigration and the prolific Hispanic birthrate, I responded, "I believe you will."

US Census statistics suggest the scavenging man was right. California, now about 37 percent Latino, is expected to be majority Hispanic by 2042. A quarter of all Americans will probably be Latino in 40 years.

This trend has worrisome aspects. Imagine a huge, growing Hispanic underclass in America with a grudge, a burning sense of having been victimized by the "gringos [term for foreigner in Latin America]."

I witnessed this grudge up close a few years ago at Texas A&M International University in Laredo. Hispanic students challenged me, claiming any restriction of illegal immigration across the US southern border with Mexico is a violation of Latinos' human rights.

Me: "Would you try to reenter Spain without a passport?"

Students: "Of course not."

Me: "What about France, or Britain?"

Students: "No."

Yet many of these illegal Latino immigrants suffer the illusion they are divinely entitled to colonize the US—and not just the states bordering Mexico, but Chicago and the East Coast as well.

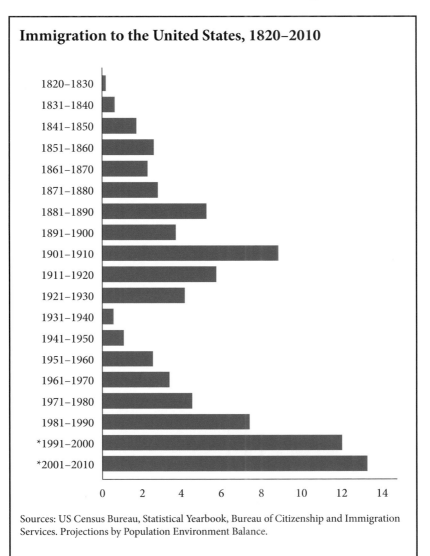

Immigration to the United States, 1820–2010

1820–1830	
1831–1840	
1841–1850	
1851–1860	
1861–1870	
1871–1880	
1881–1890	
1891–1900	
1901–1910	
1911–1920	
1921–1930	
1931–1940	
1941–1950	
1951–1960	
1961–1970	
1971–1980	
1981–1990	
*1991–2000	
*2001–2010	

Sources: US Census Bureau, Statistical Yearbook, Bureau of Citizenship and Immigration Services. Projections by Population Environment Balance.

TAKEN FROM: SUSPS, "Population Numbers, Projections, Graphs and Data," susps.org.

Some Hispanics talk openly of a *reconquista*, an effort to reclaim the American Southwest that once belonged to Mexico.

Historically, this concept is wide of the mark. Most Hispanic ancestors of immigrants owned no land. Their forebears were serfs of the Roman Catholic Church, once the largest landholder in Latin America and the world. Other ancestors labored as landless peons for Spanish colonial landlords who were later relieved of their lands by 19th-century Anglo-Americans.

Historical entitlement is but one of the myths surrounding illegal Hispanic immigration. Gringos have their own fables, such as ultimate assimilation into a greater English-speaking society.

Professor Lawrence Harrison of Tufts University in Medford, Mass., notes that "In California, fourth- and fifth-generation Mexican immigrants are still speaking only Spanish and resisting assimilation." He says there are serious cultural barriers to the old melting-pot concept. "Words like compromise and dissent, crucial concepts to American democracy, have radically different meanings in Spanish." Dissent, for example, translates into "heresy."

Most alarming, today's influx of poor Latin American immigrants comes from countries less than congenial to democracy, a law-based society, or public education. Many experts look with alarm on the fact that, unlike earlier European and Asian immigrants, the tsunami from the south too often undervalues educating children because many Hispanic parents resent the idea that their children will have more education than they have. In 2000, only 25 percent of working-age male Mexican immigrants had graduated high school, a sad fact that contributes to an increasingly volatile underclass.

Limited legal Latino immigration greatly enriches the United States. I've personally seen how Hispanic Americans bring tremendous loyalty and leadership qualities to our armed forces.

But it is morally shameful to expect taxpayers to fund free education and medical care for lawbreakers so that the wealthiest Americans—restaurant owners, ranchers, agribusiness owners, and construction companies—can hire cheap labor regardless of the national consequences.

It is ever the wealthy sticking it to the poor. With so many Americans losing their homes and unable to find jobs, it is outrageous to say Hispanics still take jobs no one else will do.

Congress, which generally represents the wealthy, should begin by imposing huge fines on affluent Americans who hire illegals. Start with the millionaires in my neighborhood, who don't mow their own lawns or baby-sit their children and instead hire immigrants who are almost certainly illegal.

Businessmen are bonkers if they think opening US borders to allow the free flow of uneducated labor will make America competitive with a burgeoning Chinese economy.

Naive American liberals need to stop trilling over [US poet] Emma Lazarus's "Give me your tired, your poor,/ Your huddled masses. . . ." World population was 1.5 billion when she penned those lines. It now approaches 7 billion. America is not a dumping ground for the rest of the world's surplus population.

Committing national suicide is not without precedent. The Dutch are rapidly losing their country. Before long, its largest cities will belong to Muslim immigrants. What then becomes of the liberal tradition of Erasmus and traditional Dutch tolerance?

Illegal immigration may ultimately be more threatening to the character and values of the US than any threat from radical Islamists. It's not about tribe; it's about the law.

| "*Many thousands of men and women have made the journey from non-citizen immigrant to citizen while fighting, and sometimes dying, in the US military.*"

Immigrants Embrace American Values

Daniel Allott

In the viewpoint that follows, Daniel Allott argues that the data suggest immigrants are not a threat to traditional American values. Allott points out that that immigrants perform better on the civics section of the US naturalization test, implying immigrants care more about understanding the traditional values of America. Other data Allott cites suggest that immigrants are less likely to break the law, are more religious, start more buinesses, and do bettter in school. Allott contends that Americans who believe immigrants are a threat to traditional values should look at the mounting evidence that suggests otherwise. Daniel Allott has written for many publications, including the Christian Science Monitor.

As you read, consider the following questions:

1. According to Allott a 2012 poll found that 35 percent of American citizens failed the civics section of the US naturalization test, while what percentage of immigrants passed the test in 2012?

2. How many thousands of noncitizens join the military every year, according to the author?

3. According the the Pew Research Center and cited by the author, what percentage of Americans believe immigrants threaten traditional American values?

A comprehensive immigration reform bill has passed the Senate, but it faces dubious prospects in the House, where it probably won't garner enough of the Republican support needed to bring it to a floor vote. One Republican sticking point is that the prospective law doesn't go far enough to ensure that immigrants integrate into American society to become productive, contributing members who uphold American values and are civically engaged.

But there is a rich irony in such concern over whether immigrants will become productive members of society: On several traditional measures of American values and societal productivity, America's native-born citizens are being outperformed by its immigrants—both legal and undocumented.

Studies show that immigrants applying for citizenship surpass American citizens on tests of knowledge of American history and civics. To take one example, in a 2012 telephone poll, Xavier University researchers found that 35 percent of Americans failed the civics section of the US naturalization test. In contrast, 97.5 percent of immigrants applying for citizenship passed the test in 2012.

The willingness to defend one's country is generally considered a reliable measure of patriotism. As General George S.

Patton once said, "The highest obligation and privilege of citizenship is that of bearing arms for one's country."

Immigrants have served with distinction in the US military in every major armed conflict since the Revolutionary War. And according to the Center for Naval Analysis, the three-month attrition rate of non-citizen soldiers is nearly twice that of US citizens.

Many thousands of men and women have made the journey from non-citizen immigrant to citizen while fighting, and sometimes dying, in the US military. The Pentagon estimates that roughly 8,000 non-citizens join the military every year, which can be a path to citizenship.

Law abidance is another basic marker of good citizenship. And studies show that both legal and illegal immigrants are less likely than the native born to break the law. That was the conclusion of a 2010 Cato Institute report, which cited a 2008 study by the Public Policy Institute of California (PPIC), the state with the highest number of immigrants. It found that "US-born men have an institutionalization rate that is 10 times higher than that of foreign-born men."

Overall, the PPIC researchers found that American-born adult men are two-and-a-half times more likely to be incarcerated than foreign-born men, including both legal and illegal immigrants. The Cato report cites Harvard sociologist Robert Sampson, who in 2006 concluded that immigrants have not increased crime in America, and that they could actually be part of the reason why crime has decreased so much.

Religiosity is also a traditional American value. In his book "Democracy in America," Alexis De Tocqueville wrote: "Religion in America . . . must be regarded as the foremost of the political institutions of that country." Legal immigrants are more religious than native-born Americans. The most important recent shift in religious observance has been the rise of the "nones"—those with no religious affiliation, whose share of the adult population reached 20 percent in 2012, according

Immigrants Pushed America to Value Ability over Social Pedigree

Compared with other societies, the United States is generally regarded as unusually competitive and placing a high premium on progress and innovation. This dynamic characteristic may well arise from the presence of immigrants and on the evolution of American institutions and identity. The size and selectivity of the immigrant community means that immigrants (and/or their children) are competing for entry into colleges, jobs, and access to prestigious positions and institutions. Not all institutions have been open to outsiders on an equal footing with insiders. In particular, high status organizations often give preference to persons with the right connections and social pedigree. But institutions that opened their doors to talented outsiders—immigrants and their children— probably gained a competitive advantage. Over time, greater openness and meritocratic processes may have become a force that shaped the evolution of American institutions in the arts, sports, science, and some sectors of business. In turn, the participation of outsiders may have reinforced a distinctive American character and culture that values not "who are you?" But, "what can you do?" . . .

The United States is a competitive society that values progress and success. This dynamic characteristic has partly been created through the presence of immigrants, which has pushed the country to value skills and ability over social pedigree.

Charles Hirschman,
Daedalus, *Summer 2013.*

to the Pew Forum. In contrast, a May 2013 Pew Forum survey found that only 14 percent of legal immigrants are religiously unaffiliated, a share that has remained relatively stable over many years.

Also, as former Florida Gov. Jeb Bush pointed out in a recent speech, immigrants' families are more likely to be intact than those of native-born Americans. According to the Census Bureau's most recent data, 39 percent of births to native-born Americans are to unwed mothers, while just 24 percent of births to foreign-born mothers are out of wedlock.

In many cases, native-born Americans aren't doing as well in school as the children of recent immigrants. A February Pew Research Center survey found that immigrants' children are more likely than the general population to have a bachelor's degree (36 percent to 31 percent). The report also found that "second-generation Hispanics and Asians place more importance than does the general public on hard work and career success."

Finally, native-born Americans start fewer businesses than immigrants. In fact, they were half as likely as foreign-born Americans to start a new business in 2011.

According to the Pew Research Center, 46 percent of Americans believe "the growing number of newcomers threaten traditional American values." But the data show otherwise. Newcomers reinforce—not undermine—American values.

Periodical and Internet Sources Bibliography

The following articles have been selected to supplement the diverse views presented in this chapter.

Lorraine Adams	"Being Muslim in America," *New Republic*, September 15, 2011.
Rich Benjamin	"Refugees of Diversity," *American Prospect*, October 2009.
Alan Ehrenhalt	"Becoming Us," *Governing*, July 2008.
John Feffer	"Running Against Islam," *Foreign Policy in Focus*, February 27, 2012.
Luis Gutiererz	"Dream Deferred," *U.S. Catholic*, August 2012.
Liz Jackson	"The New Assimilationism: The Push for 'Patriotic' Education in the United States Since September 11," *Journal for Critical Education Policy Studies*, August 2010.
Daisy Khan	"Balancing Tradition and Pluralism," *Sojourners*, February 2009.
Peter Skerry	"The Muslim-American Muddle," *National Affairs*, Fall 2011.
Richard Sobel	"Citizenship as Foundation," *TriQuarterly*, 2008.
Tim Stanley	"The Changing Face of the American Family," *History Today*, November 2012.

For Further Discussion

Chapter 1

1. The first two viewpoints in the chapter examine the impact of religious freedom on American values. Jennifer A. Marshall contends that the Founding Fathers believed religious freedom was necessary to ensure the government did not infringe on other rights of the people and that exercise of this right would help to morally guide the country. David Niose argues that the growing secularist movement in the country provides the best opportunity to check the fundamentalist element in politics. After reading these two viewpoints, do you think the country would benefit from becoming more secular, or do you think it is important to hold onto the nation's religious roots?

2. Many people have argued throughout history about the benefits and consequences that accompany capitalism. This debate continues today with Robert Ringer maintaining that capitalism is necessary for a free society and Robert J. Dewar asserting that capitalism serves only to enslave people. Reread the viewpoints and think about your own life and the lives of those around you. Do you see any points of comparison between the examples in the viewpoints and your personal examples? Discuss these examples and why you think capitalism is either good or bad for individuals and society.

Chapter 2

1. The size and reach of government is a frequent topic of debate in the United States. Steven Greenhut argues that a large government stifles freedom and prosperity, while Drew Westen claims that a large government protects the people. After reading these two arguments, on which side

of the debate do you fall? If you agree with Greenhut, try to think of any other negative impacts of a large government, and if you side with Westen, attempt to give other benefits.

2. Recently implemented government policies have raised questions about whether the United States is moving toward a socialist form of government, which in turn has sparked debate as to whether socialism and American values are compatible. Jedediah Purdy contends that socialism and American values are not inherently opposed. After reading this viewpoint, construct your own opinion as to whether an American socialism can exist. As you make your argument, either for or against an American socialism, use specific examples from the viewpoint as well as your own.

3. Doug Bandow claims that welfare states are unfair and create dependent citizens. Arloc Sherman, Robert Greenstein, and Kathy Ruffing, however, use statistics to show that welfare goes to the people who need it most, and this is not inconsistent with American values. Which tactic do you find more convincing? Do Bandow's examples add credibility to his argument? Do the statistics employed by Sherman, Greenstein, and Ruffing convince you that only the people most in need receive welfare? Include specific examples from the viewpoints as you make your case.

4. A recent survey by the Pew Research Center revealed that women have become the primary or sole breadwinners in 40 percent of American households. These findings have led some to conclude that this is a positive trend for both women and Americans as a whole, but others have suggested that this signals the trend of declining American family values. *The Economist* viewpoint falls in the first camp, while Selwyn Duke falls in the latter. After reading over the findings of the survey and the viewpoints of both authors, with whom do you agree more, or is there a

third view not represented by either of these viewpoints? Explain your answer, citing the authors for support or giving other examples that refute their claims.

Chapter 3

1. Since the terrorist attacks on September 11, 2001, took place in New York City and the ensuing wars commenced, the question of what constitutes patriotism in the United States has been debated numerous times. Jose Cespedes argues that patriotism and American values are closely linked, and that embracing American values is a patriotic act. In contrast, Matthew Rothschild argues against acts of patriotism, contending that they lead to rifts between people, violence, and death. After reading both viewpoints, with whom do you agree more? Should Americans be patriotic? Why or why not? Use quotes from the viewpoints to support your claims.

2. For many American students, the school day begins with a group recitation of the Pledge of Allegiance, but not everyone believes this should be the case. Erik Nielson argues that the pledge's history reveals its recitation is not a patriotic gesture, only nationalistic and religious indoctrination. Ernest Smartt maintains that teaching not only the Pledge of Allegiance but patriotism itself in schools would improve the nation. Think about your own experiences in school. Did you recite the Pledge of Allegiance every day? Was patriotism a topic discussed in any of your classes? Do you think the presence or lack of discussion on this topic improved or stifled your knowledge and understanding of the country? Use specific examples from your experience in your answer.

3. Support for American troops is often considered one of the highest forms of patriotism. Ronnie Polaneczky contends that supporting the troops provides a cause around which all Americans can unify. Jacob G. Hornberger con-

trasts this view in his argument that supporting the troops creates a risk for the well-being of all Americans. Whose viewpoint do you find more persuasive? Can you find any flaws in the viewpoint of the author with whom you disagree? Include quotes from the viewpoints to clarify your statements.

Chapter 4

1. Amil Imani argues that political correctness has created a situation where Americans are unable or refuse to see that Islam and American values cannot coexist, using quotes from the Quran and examples of practices deriving from Islam. Matthew Duss, on the other hand, contends that individuals who exhibit anti-Islamic sentiment are the ones who stand in opposition to American values. Which author do you believe presents a more believable argument? What examples or points are most convincing, and why? Cite these examples and explain their importance in determining your own view. Also consider how your knowledge of the First Amendment right to religious freedom impacts your view.

Organizations to Contact

The editors have compiled the following list of organizations concerned with the issues debated in this book. The descriptions are derived from materials provided by the organizations. All have publications or information available for interested readers. The list was compiled on the date of publication of the present volume; the information provided here may change. Be aware that many organizations take several weeks or longer to respond to inquiries, so allow as much time as possible.

Alliance Defending Freedom
15100 N. 90th Street, Scottsdale, AZ   85260
(800) 835-233 • fax (480) 444-0025
website: www.alliancedefendingfreedom.org

Alliance Defending Freedom is a nonprofit organization dedicated to spreading the word of the Bible, pushing for change in the legal system, and advancing religious liberty, the sanctity of life, and marriage and family. The Alliance was founded by a group of Christian leaders around the nation who found religious freedom in the country to be eroding, specifically from continued attacks by the American Civil Liberties Union. This organization has worked to combat those attacks with detailed information about its activities available on the Alliance's website along with access to the organization's publication *Faith and Justice.*

American Civil Liberties Union (ACLU)
125 Broad Street, 18th Floor, New York, NY   10004
(212) 549-2500
website: www.aclu.org

The ACLU is a national organization working on behalf of all Americans to protect First Amendment free speech, assembly, press, and religion rights, equal protection under the law, due process rights, and privacy. The organization's efforts are particularly focused on groups whose rights have historically been underrepresented—people of color, women, LGBT populations, and people with disabilities. The ACLU website contains articles with overviews of the American values guarded by the organization and actions being taken to ensure their continued protection. Broad headings include Keep America Safe and Free and Protecting Civil Liberties in the Digital Age.

American Enterprise Institute (AEI)

1150 17th Street NW, Washington, DC   20036
(202) 862-5800 • fax (202) 862-7177
website: www.aei.org

AEI is a private, nonpartisan, nonprofit public policy think tank that conducts research on topics pertaining to government, politics, economics, and social welfare and provides educational materials about the findings to the public and policy makers to drive policy change. The main ideals promoted by the organization include the expansion of liberty, the advancement of individual opportunity, and the support of free enterprise. AEI explores these American values in several areas of policy studies, including economics, foreign and defense policy, politics and public opinion, health, education, energy and the environment, and society and culture. Articles on these topics as well as pieces from *The American*, the official online magazine of AEI, can be read on the organization's website.

American Humanist Association

1777 T Street NW, Washington, DC   20009-7125
(202) 238-9088 • fax (202) 238-9003
website: www.americanhumanist.org

AHA was worked for more than seventy years to improve society through the promotion of nontheism combined with strong ethical values that advance kindness and scientific understanding of the world. Through its publishing activities, conferences, and outreach work, the organization seeks to inform everyone that religion is not what makes people good.

The Humanist is the bimonthly magazine of the organization, and its articles, as well as *Free Mind*, the AHA's quarterly newsletter, can be accessed on the AHA website.

American Values
PO Box 1223, Merrifield, VA   22116-1223
(703) 671-9700 • fax (703) 671-1680
e-mail: gary.bauer@amvalues.org
website: www.ouramericanvalues.org

American Values is a nonprofit organization dedicated to promoting the values of the Founding Fathers, specifically faith in democracy, family, and freedom. The organization's website provides stories grouped into three main categories—life, marriage, and Israel—along with access to the End of Day Archives, which contains observations about current issues. Video archives present short overviews of topics relating to American values.

Cato Institute
1000 Massachusetts Ave. NW, Washington, DC   20001-5403
(202) 842-0200
website: www.cato.org

Cato is a libertarian public policy think tank committed to promoting policy that advances the values of personal freedom, limited government, free enterprise, and peace. Cato research includes government and politics, heath care and welfare, law and civil liberties, and trade and immigration, among many others. Articles such as "Do Immigrants Undermine American Values?" and "Federal Marriage Amendment Is Contrary to American Values" can be read on the Cato website.

Center for American Progress
1333 H Street NW, 10th Floor, Washington, DC   20005
(202) 682-1611
website: www.americanprogress.org

The Center for American Progress is an independent, nonpartisan public policy research organization that seeks to advance American society through the promotion of progressive ideas.

The organization's main courses of action include advocating for new progressive policy, critiquing conservative policy, pushing the media to report on issues that matter most to American people, and forming the national conversation on these issues. The center covers a range of topics, including civil liberties, health care, immigration, and women's rights among many others. Articles and reports on these and other American values can be read on the Center for American Progress website.

Future of Freedom Foundation (FFF)
11350 Random Hills Road, Suite 800, Fairfax, VA   22030
(703) 934-6101 • fax (703) 352-8678
e-mail: fff@fff.org
website: www.fff.org

FFF has worked since its founding in 1989 to advance libertarian ideals on a national level. These ideals include individual freedom, free markets, private property, and limited government. FFF publishes a range of articles and provides an archive of past publications on its website. Titles relating to American values include "Edward Snowden and the Corruption of Morals and Values," "The Evil of the National-Security State," and "Do Republicans Oppose the Redistribution of Wealth?"

Heritage Foundation
214 Massachusetts Ave. NE, Washington, DC   20002-4999
(202) 546-4400
e-mail: info@heritage.org
website: www.heritage.org

The Heritage Foundation is a national, public policy research organization that espouses the conservative values of limited government, free markets, personal freedom, traditional American values, and a strong national defense. This organization conducts research on pertinent policy issues and disseminates the findings to policy makers, the media, and academic communities to drive national debate and promote policy change. Heritage publishes numerous reports, back-grounders, podcasts, and transcripts of events on all topics, including American values, with titles including "American Values, Immigrants, and Land of Opportunity," "Still the Best Hope: Why the World Needs American Values to Triumph," and "Women's Treaty Still Threatens American Rights and Values." These and many others can be accessed on the Heritage website.

People for the American Way (PFAW)
1101 15th Street NW, Suite 600, Washington, DC   20005
(202) 467-4999
website: www.pfaw.org

PFAW is a national organization that seeks to ensure that all Americans experience equality, freedom of speech, freedom of religion, the right to pursue justice through the court system, and the right to vote. Additionally, the organization works to combat the extreme ideology they believe the religious Right is imposing on the country. Articles on these topics, including "Citizenship in the Balance: How Anti-Immigrant Activists Twist the Facts, Ignore History, and Flout the Constitution," "Schools and Censorship: Banned Books," and "Religious Protection Laws in the United States," can be read on the PFAW website.

Bibliography of Books

Andrew Bacevich   *Breach of Trust: How Americans
                    Failed Their Soldiers and Their
                    Country*. New York: Metropolitan,
                    2013.

Edwin Feulner   *The American Spirit: Celebrating the
and Brian Tracy   Virtues and Values That Make Us
                    Great*. Nashville: Thomas Nelson,
                    2012.

Morris P. Fiorina *Culture War? The Myth of a Polarized
with Samuel J.   America*. New York: Longman, 2010.
Abrams and
Jeremy C. Pope

Dana Frank   *Buy American: The Untold Story of
                    Economic Nationalism*. Boston:
                    Beacon, 2000.

Robert P. George   *Conscience and Its Enemies:
                    Confronting the Dogmas of Our Age*.
                    Wilmington, DE: ISI Books, 2013.

William Greider   *Come Home, America: The Rise and
                    Fall (and Redeeming Promise) of Our
                    Country*. New York: Rodale, 2009.

Yvonne Yazbeck   *Muslim Women in America: The
Haddad, Jane I.   Challenge of Islamic Identity Today*.
Smith, and   New York: Oxford University Press,
Kathleen M.   2006.
Moore

Bill Ong Hing   *Deporting Our Souls: Values, Morality,
                    and Immigration Policy*. New York:
                    Cambridge University Press, 2006.

James Davison Hunter — *Culture Wars: The Struggle to Control the Family, Art, Education, Law, and Politics in America.* New York: Basic Books, 1991.

Stephen P. Kiernan — *Authentic Patriotism: Restoring America's Founding Ideals Through Selfless Action.* New York: St. Martin's, 2010.

George Lakoff — *Thinking Points: Communicating Our American Values and Vision.* New York: Farrar, Straus and Giroux, 2006.

Jeffrey Lang — *Even Angels Ask: A Journey to Islam in America.* Beltsville, MD: Amana, 1997.

Phillip Longman — *Return of Thrift: How the Collapse of the Middle Class Welfare State Will Reawaken Values in America.* New York: Free Press, 1996.

John Mackey and Rajendra Sisodia — *Conscious Capitalism: Liberating the Heroic Spirit of Business.* Boston: Harvard Business School, 2013.

Andrew C. McCarthy — *The Grand Jihad: How Islam and the Left Sabotage America.* New York: Encounter, 2010.

Richard McCormack, ed. — *Manufacturing a Better Future for America.* Washington, DC: Alliance for American Manufacturing, 2005.

Charles Murray	*American Exceptionalism: An Experiment in History.* Washington, DC: American Enterprise Institute Press, 2013.
Barack Obama	*The Audacity of Hope: Thoughts on Reclaiming the American Dream.* New York: Random House, 2006.
Brad O'Leary	*The Audacity of Deceit: Barack Obama's War on American Values.* Los Angeles: WND, 2008.
Dennis Prager	*Still the Best Hope: Why the World Needs American Values to Triumph.* New York: HarperCollins, 2012.
Michael A. Santoro and Ronald J. Strauss	*Wall Street Values: Business Ethics and the Global Financial Crisis.* New York: Cambridge University Press, 2013.
David Sehat	*The Myth of American Religious Freedom.* New York: Oxford University Press, 2011.
Robert Sirico	*Defending the Free Market: The Moral Case for a Free Economy.* Washington, DC: Regnery, 2012.
Jim Wallis	*Rediscovering Values: On Wall Street, Main Street, and Your Street.* New York: Howard, 2010.
Writers for the 99%	*Occupying Wall Street: The Inside Story of an Action That Changed America.* New York: OR Books, 2012.

Index

A

B